Napoleon and Betsy

RECOLLECTIONS OF NAPOLEON ON ST HELENA

SAINTE HÉLÈNE

Échelle de 1:85.000e

0   1   2   3   4 Km.

OCÉAN ATLANTIQUE

Sugar Loaf pt.   5°40 Ouest de Greenwich

Barn Long Point

The Barn

Prosperous Bay

Saddle pt.

Gill Point

Flagstaff Bay

Flagstaff Hill

Plateau et Camp de Deadwood

DEADWOOD

New House

Old House

Plateau de Longwood

LONGWOOD

Fisher's

Valley

16°

5°40

Munden's pt.

JAMESTOWN

Ladder Hill (Fort)

Mess des Officiers

Briers

High Knoll Fort

Rupert torrent

Sénégambie

Punch du Diable

Tombeau

Hut's Gate

Pic de Diane

Rock Rose Hill

Powell pt.

PLANTATION HOUSE

CATHÉDRALE

Rosemary

Doveton Mont Pleasant

Chapelle Baptista

S A N D Y   B A Y

Sandy Bay

Castle Rock pt.

Pointe Sud Ouest

16°

Napoleon and Betsy

RECOLLECTIONS OF NAPOLEON ON ST HELENA

LUCIA ELIZABETH ABELL
(BETSY BALCOMBE)

EDITED WITH A NEW INTRODUCTION
BY ALAN SUTTON

FONTHILL

Fonthill Media Limited
www.fonthillmedia.com

This edition published in the United Kingdom 2012

British Library Cataloguing in Publication Data:
A catalogue record for this book is available from the British Library

ISBN 978-1-78155-034-2 (PRINT)
ISBN 978-1-78155-135-6 (E-BOOK)

New colour photographs of St Helena reproduced with kind
permission of John Tyrrell. For general information on St Helena visit
John's blog: http://johntyrrell.blogspot.com

Typeset in 10pt on 14pt Sabon
Printed and bound in England

Connect with us
facebook.com/fonthillmedia   twitter.com/fonthillmedia

EDITORIAL NOTE
TO THE 2012 EDITION

The text, with its naivety and inconsistencies has, in large, been left as it was. Some original typesetting errors have been corrected (and probably some new ones introduced!) and spelling has been modernised to a slight, but not total extent. The redundant poetry at the beginning of each chapter has been removed, but this apart; the text is as Elizabeth Abell presented it. The few literary embellishments within the text have been retained.

New notes have been added to provide a more detailed background to the numerous people mentioned in the book, and some of the notes provide basic translations where deemed necessary. I have not translated the more obvious French expressions which from their context speak for themselves. Finally, many additional illustrations are included to accompany the lithograph from Elizabeth Abell's original 1844 edition.

Alan Sutton
January 2012

ACKNOWLEDGEMENTS

Since beginning this project I have been surprised at the enthusiasm with which it has been met. Betsy's book was a bestseller in its day going through several editions and yet in recent years it has largely been overlooked. The tale of how a fallen Emperor became the best friend of an English schoolgirl at first seems unlikely, and yet it is not the work of fiction. Betsy's friendship was well recorded in all contemporary narratives and it does seem if something very special existed between them. Napoleon was fond of children, and it seems that Betsy's wild, irreverent tomboy spirit struck a chord. Napoleon's staff were at first horrified about her antics in his presence, but later, at Longwood, even they began to use Betsy as a method of 'cheering up' their Emperor.

For help with colour illustrations I wish to thank John Tyrell for his scenic shots of St Helena, and for advice on the source of some old black and white engravings and line drawings. I thank Michel Dancoisne-Martineau for kindly answering questions and supplying information. The booklet produced by the Briars Park, Mt Martha, Victoria, Australia has also been of much assistance. For the fascinating water-colours made by Denzil Ibbetson I am very grateful to Hamish Coney, Managing Director of Art & Object, Newton, Auckland, New Zealand. For the aquatints made from illustrations by George Hutchins Bellasis I am very grateful to Barry Weaver.

Alan Sutton

INTRODUCTION
TO THE 2012 EDITION

The Balcombe Family

Lucia Elizabeth Abell, née Balcombe, was baptised on 26 November 1802 at St James, Clerkenwell, the second daughter of William Balcombe, (1779-1829), an ex-naval officer, and his wife Jane, née Cranston. William and Jane had been settled at Swallowfield, Reading, and took up residence at St Helena in 1805. In addition to his official position with the Honourable East India Company as superintendent of public sales, William was a merchant in partnership with William Fowler and Joseph Cole; the principal business of the firm being that of purveyors to the various ships, mainly H.E.I.C. vessels, touching at Jamestown.

The eldest child of the family was Jane, (1800-1824), and it was therefore a young family of four that migrated to St Helena. Once settled there, the family was added to with the arrival of three sons; William, (1808-1852); Thomas Tyrwhitt, (1810-1861) and Alexander Beatson, (1811-1877).

On 15 October 1815, HMS *Northumberland* arrived at the island with Napoleon and his entourage, and three days later he took up his residence in a small pavilion in the garden of the Balcombe's house, "The Briars". This was enlarged on a temporary basis by the addition of a marquee. He remained there until his removal to Longwood on 10 December 1815. Why he stayed at Briars is unclear, but it seems that Napoleon's own wishes on the subject may have had something to do with it.

HMS *Icarus* had arrived at St Helena a few days before *Northumberland* arrived, but the Governor had not had time to digest the consequences or to fully consider the accommodation requirements. When *Northumberland* arrived, Admiral Cockburn himself appears uncertain as to where Napoleon was to stay. Maps he had been given indicated that Plantation House was to be considered, but it was all less than clear and presumably Government left it to be decided by Cockburn and the Governor. Cockburn had hoped for Plantation House — the Governor's house — but Sir Mark Wilks, the

Governor, studiously avoided any mention of a change and was clearly unwilling to give up his comfortable home. Therefore, the first night after arrival, Napoleon and his entourage remained on board ship. The next day, at dusk, the party landed to be met by curious by-standing islanders. That night the entourage remained at a boarding house kept at James Town by Henry Porteous, Superintendent of H.E.I.C.'s gardens.

It is assumed that Longwood was a suggestion put forward by Sir Mark Wilks. The next day Admiral Cockburn arranged for Napoleon to ride with him to Longwood, and in going and returning they passed the Briars, and that appears to have been that. Napoleon enquired about the bungalow in its pleasant gardens, and Cockburn, already acquainted with William Balcombe, arranged the introduction. From that point on everything was quickly arranged. The Emperor would stay at the Briars on a temporary basis with a few key members of his staff, and the others of the entourage would remain at James Town.

William Balcombe and his family were frequently hosts, and the Balcombe's pavilion housed many guests over the years. The Duke of Wellington, as Major-General Sir Arthur Wellesley, stayed in the pavilion at the Briars on a stop-over of a few days on his return from India in 1805. Many years later when Wellington heard that his friend Admiral Sir Pulteney Malcolm was about to go to St Helena he sent him the following letter:

PARIS, APRIL 3rd, 1816.

My Dear Malcolm,

I am very much obliged to you for Mr. Simpson's book which I will read when I shall have a moment's leisure. I am glad you have taken command at St Helena, upon which I congratulate you. You must never be idle if you can avoid it.

You may tell 'Bony' that I find his apartments at the Elysée Bourbon very convenient and that I hope he likes mine at Mr. Balcombe's. It is a droll sequel enough to the affairs of Europe that we should change places of residence.

I am yours most sincerely,
WELLINGTON.

Whether Sir Pulteney actually forwarded the message to 'Bony' is not known, but he did strike up a good relationship with Napoleon, and Lady Malcolm frequently played chess with the Emperor. Given that Sir Pulteney was very tactful in his relations with Napoleon, It may be assumed that he chose not to pass on that particular message!

The chosen residence for Napoleon was therefore to be Longwood; formerly the summer residence of the Lieutenant Governor, but this required conversion for the use of Napoleon and his staff. In fact Longwood had originally been built as a cattle barn and storage shed. It was converted in 1812 to a summer residence by the Lieutenant-Governor at the time, Mark Wilks. This was accomplished by laying floor boards over the dirt and dried cow dung, and by installing drop ceilings. The house was rebuilt and expanded to accommodate Napoleon and his party by British naval carpenters under the supervision of Admiral George Cockburn, but rats still infested the house (a large rat even jumping out of Napoleon's hat when he was about to put it on). Even today, the French Government, which owns the property, is unable to get rid of the smell of damp from the house; and during his years there, Napoleon felt the location was conducive to rheumatism.

At the Briars, Napoleon at once showed an interest in William Balcombe's younger daughter Betsy, and his fondness for this child is one of the most pleasing episodes in the history of the captivity. Balcombe owed the appointment of his firm as purveyors to Longwood to the intimacy which existed between Napoleon and his family. On account of these friendly relations, the Balcombes frequently visited the Emperor there, and on a number of occasions were included in the company at dinner.

The close business alliance between Balcombe and the residents at Longwood aroused the suspicion of the new Governor, Sir Hudson Lowe, and it became evident to the purveyor that it would not be safe to remain in St Helena much longer. A much more detailed account of the difficult relationship between Sir Hudson Lowe and William Balcombe is given in another Fonthill title: *Napoleon on St Helena* by Mabel Brookes. Mabel was Betsy's grand-niece, as explained below.

William Balcombe appears to have been a convivial character and had influential friends. He certainly hosted many important people at his table and was fond of his drink. His ability as an administrator is more questionable. William Balcombe left the Island with his family in the *Winchelsea* on 18 March 1818, and soon after his departure Lowe received proof of his suspicion that Balcombe had been acting as an intermediary in the transmission of clandestine correspondence to Europe, and in negotiating bills drawn by Napoleon. As a consequence, it became impossible for him to return, although he frequently petitioned Lord Bathurst, the British Minister responsible for the safe-keeping of Napoleon, to be allowed to do so. During all of this period of petitioning, William Balcombe and his family remained in England, living chiefly at Chudleigh, Devon. Balcombe suffered from a dwindling income, acute gout and continual fear of punishment due to his actions. Eventually, in 1823, Sir Hudson Lowe relented.

The exact reasons are unclear, but it is known that the elder daughter, Jane, using influential parliamentary friends, managed to apply some pressure in appropriate places. It also appears that Balcombe had been approached by Lowe, as a result of which he filed an affidavit in Lowe's favour, in the legal dispute between Sir Hudson Lowe and Dr Barry O'Meara, the physician who had the responsibility of attending Napoleon. This favourable affidavit probably induced Lowe to withdraw the objections he had steadily made to Balcombe's advancement. In the *Lowe Papers*, volume 20, p. 233, there is a letter from Balcombe, dated 1823, in which he expresses the hope that Sir Hudson will now 'overlook any differences that may have existed'.

It had taken William Balcombe five years to restore his standing with the Government, exerting every connection he and his family had. Rumours persisted that he was the illegitimate son of the Prince Regent who, in 1820, was crowned George IV. If he had been, he would have been the result of a very early 'fling', for the Prince would only have been sixteen-years-old at the time, and if William's elder brother was from the same sire, the Prince would have been 'active' in extreme youth. Certainly Balcombe had an influential patron in Sir Thomas Tyrwhitt, who formerly had been private secretary to the Prince, and who for many years was Gentleman Usher of the Black Rod in the House of Lords. Balcombe's second son was named after him. It does seem that this rumour of illegitimacy was without firm foundation, but it was in wide circulation on St Helena and provided William Balcombe with some *cachet* — which he appears to have done little to dispel. Sir Hudson Lowe knew of the rumour, and he appears to have been somewhat on his guard in case untoward pressure came from the quarter of St James's. Had it not been for this hesitance, Lowe may well have acted sooner and pre-empted Balcombe's departure. The rumour came about because William and his elder brother spent much time at Carlton House during their young life, and were provided with a privileged education. The official line is that he and his brother were educated by the King's Bounty — their purported father, captain of a frigate, having reputedly been lost at sea with his ship. Apparently it was the standard procedure in those days for such sons to be assisted in their schooling by such means. That said that, if all sons of officers lost at sea were privileged with accommodation at Carlton House, it would have become very crowded.

One other unsubstantiated suggestion is that his father may have been killed in an accident for which a member of the Royal Family was responsible. Whatever the truth of the matter, it is without doubt that the connection with Sir Thomas Tyrwhitt is substantial. As well as his connections to the Prince Regent, Tyrwhitt was a powerful man in Devon. He was the founder of what became Dartmoor Prison (Prince Town), and he was close enough to the Balcombe family to attend Betsy Balcombe's wedding.

William's elder brother, a soldier, remained equerry to the Regent for many years and eventually retired as Inspector-General of Yeomanry about 1847.

William's lot as a sailor held more in it of drama. He began his naval career in 1795 as clerk to Captain Sotheron on HMS *Romney*. Hot-tempered and impulsive, he later fell foul of a superior officer by refusing to transmit his order for a flogging which he considered unjust, and, but for the Prince's intervention, he would have been summarily cashiered. Beyond this, little is known, and although Royal illegitimacy remains a possibility, it is questionable and surrounded in a mist. It should be added that if it were true, it might have taken less than five years for William to obtain a further official position.

* * *

As a result of the concerted efforts, William Balcombe was favoured with a Colonial post and the Colonial Government in New South Wales provided him with a handsome house in Sydney and an extensive land grant at Bungonia, some 120 miles to the south-west. With his family he arrived at Sydney in April 1824 on board the *Hibernia*. His elder daughter Jane died on the voyage and Betsy, who had married Edward Abell, a handsome man-about-town, and who had been temporarily deserted by him, was with them. In 1826 Betsy received a letter from George Heathcote (who had been a young naval officer at St Helena on HMS *Conqueror*). The letter was dated from Edinburgh, 25 March 1826, and was presumably delivered to Australia about June or July 1826. In this letter George writes:

> *"Mr Stokoe has just been here, sends his kind love and desires me to say he is thinking of going to Joseph Bonaparte in America. He was extremely distressed at the news of poor Jane's death.*
>
> *His feelings however had not been so dreadful as mine for after I had mourned for you, dearest Betsy, I had to lament the loss of Jane — God bless you and preserve you.*

Dearest Betsy, where is this husband who I heard treated you so cruelly? Do you feel lawfully bound to him still?

What is his name and where does he live? — Forgive me, dearest Betsy, if in asking these questions I hurt your better feelings and believe me I do it with more affection than you can conceive and my love for you and yours must plead my excuse . . .

I want to hear about my young friends Alex and Tom, who now, I suppose, don't remember me. They would not remember reading by my bedside in the home at Arnos Vale.

But they cannot forget that beautiful vale itself, where their young limbs were strengthened by climbing the mountainous sides — nor can Betsy forget how often in her 'more gentle' moods! she knocked me down on the grass, flat, and delighted herself with my weakness and her own strength . . ."

John Stokoe had been the surgeon on *Conqueror* and had paid court to Jane, and presumably held out future hopes. On a medical basis he attended Napoleon for three days in 1819, and on Sir Hudson Lowe finding out that his orders relating to attendance on Napoleon had been flouted, his attitude was unduly harsh. Poor Stokoe ended by being dismissed the Navy on half-pay on Lowe's demand. He was court martialled in a process that was little more than a kangaroo court. The orders he was found to have flouted were those of Admiral Plampin.

George, as it seems, had been fond of Betsy, but her diary shows that the feelings were not reciprocated. Young Ensign Heathcote had been forced to remain at Arnos Vale, a convalescent depot, on St Helena, suffering from hepatitis, the while his ship, *Conqueror*, beat around the island on guard duty. Arnos Vale, a hollow between steep cliffs, lay three miles from the Briars. The Balcombe girls visited him there bringing fruit from the garden and Jane came to read to him; thus the reference in his letter to his weakness.

It is not clear what Betsy wrote back, if she did write back, for nothing more was heard. However, whether it was prompted by this letter or from other causes, Betsy soon afterwards sailed back to England and once more took up with her wayward husband.

Betsy had married Edward Abell, (1805-1850), in Exmouth on 28 May 1822, but the relationship was unstable and there are conflicting reports, but the general consensus is that he married for money, and was presumably disappointed in finding that there was none. Why they married so young is unknown, and being minors, parental permission would have been required from both sets of parents. Edward would have been merely sixteen or seventeen at the time. Was there an indiscretion which made it necessary for them to marry? This is mere conjecture, but in best Austenesque style it remains a possibility. However, Betsy did return to him, and they did live together for a short time, and their daughter, Jane Elizabeth Balcombe Abell was born in 1827.

It seems likely that soon after young Jane was born, Betsy returned to her family — yet another exhausting, and expensive 17-week journey. Once there she was quickly back in society and Betsy, very lively and precocious, was well known as "the beautiful Mrs Abell" and was appointed to a Committee under the Governor's wife which arranged schooling for girl orphans, as young as seven, to train as servants.

In 1826 or 1827 — presumably while Betsy was absent in England — William Balcombe was embroiled in a scandal involving his deposit of Treasury funds in the insecure Bank of New South Wales. He received a formal rebuke from Whitehall which contributed to his declining health. He died at Sydney on 19 March 1829, leaving his affairs in disorder. Creditors took most of his livestock, and his widow, left only with his land grants, petitioned for a pension without success. Not to be outdone, Mrs Jane Balcombe sailed to London in 1831, with Betsy and her young daughter, to directly petition the Colonial Secretary, referring to the great losses and financial ruin William suffered because he was prohibited from returning to St Helena. While recognising the losses, the Colonial Office only awarded money grants to cover their passages to England and back to Sydney, but included a recommendation to the New South Wales Governor to consider government posts for the three young sons. The Governor advised this was not practicable as the eldest son William was content to be on the land, Alexander had been dismissed from the Commissariat for negligence, but Thomas, under consideration to be dismissed by the Surveyor General, would be retained as a Survey draftsman.

While they were in London in 1832, Betsy had contact with Joseph Bonaparte, recently arrived there following a sixteen-year exile in America. Betsy's daughter Jane remembered sitting on Joseph's knee as a young girl while he and Betsy reminisced about Napoleon, and of Joseph giving Betsy a cameo ring, said to be from Egypt, from his finger. She also appears to have met several others of the Bonaparte family, including Lucien.

Charles Louis-Napoleon Bonaparte, later to become Napoleon III, was also a frequent visitor to Betsy's home and at the end of the third edition of her *Recollections*, she intimates that Louis frequently questioned her about the personal appearance of his uncle. Did he, Louis, resemble him in any point? Had he a mannerism, 'a look'? He sought knowledge of any trivial attribute that resembled his own. Had his features at least the mould of Napoleon? Had he not the same bearing, the same air? The resolutely truthful Betsy, unchanged even in later years, was compelled to disappoint him, to tell him plainly that in no way did he resemble the Emperor. . . . Not his eyes, nor his figure; not his height . . . Perhaps his hair? She fetched the lock that had been cut by Marchand and compared it; remarkably fine and silky hair, pale in colour, with a reddish undertone. Louis succeeded in achieving some slight resemblance by brushing his own in the same manner.

* * *

On their return voyage to Sydney in 1833, seventeen-year-old Edward Eyre was a fellow first-class passenger and much enamoured of Betsy, then about 31. His autobiography includes many references to her, including a note that "Mrs Abell was in the prime of life, regular and pretty in features, commanding inform a good figure — stylish in her dress and having a strange mixture of high polish and dash in her manner which was very captivating. She had beautiful hair, a rich nut brown shot with gold in unusual fashion and of an extraordinary length." Edward went on to become a famous explorer in Australia.

Back in New South Wales Jane Balcombe and Betsy still had financial problems, and William's farm was far from Sydney and basic, so they sailed back to England in 1834, leaving the three boys in Australia. It is thought that Jane, then in her 60s and in ill health for years, went to a sister in Yorkshire, and died before civil registration of deaths started in 1837.

Of Betsy's brothers, they all remained in Australia and William, the eldest, died at the Turon goldfields in 1852. Thomas Tyrwhitt had an unsuccessful business career, but by 1837 he had won considerable repute as an artist. In 1840 he married Lydia Stuckey and they had three children, but in 1858, the death of his eldest daughter led him to suffer from bouts of mental illness. Despite this serious affliction, he managed to hold onto his position as a government surveyor and the family endured three years of frequent threats of suicide. He eventually succeeded in October 1861 by shooting himself in the head at his home, Napoleon Cottage, Paddington, New South Wales.

The third brother, Alexander, married Emma Juana Reid, of Inverary Park. He bought livestock and took his wife to Port Phillip in 1842. In 1846 he took over a property named Chen Chen Gurruck, or Tichingorourke, changing the name to 'The Briars'. In the 1850s he joined the search for gold and later settled down to the pastoral pursuits and the life of a country squire. He was appointed a magistrate in 1855 and he also experimented unsuccessfully with wine production. He died on 21 September 1877 at his home, Eastcourt, East Melbourne.

* * *

In England Betsy earned some money by teaching music and then settled down to write her book. She first published her account of *Recollections of Napoleon* in serialized form in the *New Century Magazine* in 1843, and then in book form in 1844. The book was something of a bestseller at the time; it was reprinted three times and a French edition was eventually published in 1898.

After Louis Napoleon was crowned Emperor Napoleon III in 1852, Betsy made representations to him and she was awarded with 500 hectares of land with vineyards in Algeria 'in memory of her comfort to his uncle'. It is unclear if she, herself, visited France to make the representations, or whether it was by communication, or alternatively via a third party. It is also unclear what happened to this land; for it seems unlikely that she ever visited it.

Betsy's daughter, Jane Elizabeth Balcombe Abell, married, 22 November 1848, at Stoke Damerel, Plymouth, Charles Edwards Johnstone, (1826-1868), son of George Johnstone and Margaret Anne Johnstone. There do not appear to have been children from the marriage. In the 1861 census, Charles is listed as a 'landed proprietor', and he and Jane, with his mother-in-law Betsy lived at 19 Upper Berkeley Street, Marylebone. In the 1871 census both Betsy and her daughter were widows, living together at 6 Victoria Square Westminster. Betsy died on 29 June 1871, and Jane died in 1892.

The family connection with St Helena was brought full circle in 1957 when William Balcombe's great-granddaughter, Alexander's granddaughter, Dame Mabel Brookes, visited St Helena. She purchased the Briars site and the Pavilion where Napoleon had stayed and, in 1959, in a ceremony at Malmaison in Paris, she deeded it to the French nation. The Briars is now one of the French Domains of St Helena along with Longwood House and the Tomb.

The Island of St Helena

St Helena is only a fraction larger than Jersey in the Channel Islands, but unlike Jersey it has a dramatic mountainous landscape; the result of the volcanic eruptions that created it seven million years ago.

The island was uninhabited when discovered by the Portuguese in 1502. It was first occupied, fortified and garrisoned by the British in 1658 and it is now Britain's second oldest remaining colony after Bermuda. It is one of the most isolated islands in the world. For centuries, it was an important stop-over for ships sailing to Europe from Asia and South Africa, a vital link with India and much used by H.E.I.C. — the Honourable East India Company. It was run by the Company from 1658-1834 apart from the period of Napoleon's Captivity when the Crown took it over and appointed its own Governor. The big families on the island who had dominated under the H.E.I.C. were effectively sidelined for the duration, and like nearly everyone else on the island had rather strained relations with Sir Hudson Lowe. St Helena became a crown colony in 1834. In 1981 it became a "British Dependent Territory".

St Helena's importance declined after the opening of the Suez Canal in 1869. The island is extremely remote — the nearest landmass being distant some 1,200 miles away. Its actual location is 15° 56' south 5° 43' west and it lies approximately one-third of the way west between Africa and South America, and 1,100 miles south of the Equator. In dimensions, the island is some ten miles by five miles; forty-seven square miles.

The population in 2012 is approximately 4,200, but in 1820 it was almost double, being 7,998. This was made up as follows:

Whites	3,534
Slaves	1,156
Chinese	481
Free Blacks	613
Lascars	33
	5,817
British troops	1,488
H.E.I.C.'s troops	698
	2,181
Total Population	7,998

Napoleon at Longwood

HMS *Northumberland* arrived at Jamestown, St Helena, on 15 October 1815, and three days later Napoleon and his immediate entourage were temporarily housed at a pavilion adjoining the Briars, the home of the Balcombe family. Napoleon remained here until Longwood was ready for him, 10 December 1815. Longwood was an inconvenient and uncomfortable house and Napoleon disliked it after the sheltered position of the Briars. Despite not being on good terms with Napoleon, the Governor, Sir Hudson Lowe proposed to Lord Bathurst in February 1818 to move Napoleon to Rosemary Hall, a house that became available and was located in a more hospitable part of the island, sheltered from the winds and shaded, as Napoleon had preferred. But the revelations of General Gourgaud in London brought Lord Bathurst to the opinion that it was safer to keep Napoleon at Longwood, where an escape was harder to undertake. So the building of a new house only began in October 1818, three years after Napoleon's arrival on the island. It was completed at the end of his life, but he disliked it and refused to be moved there.

Following Napoleon's death, Longwood House reverted to the East India Company and later to the Crown, and was used for agricultural purposes as a granary. Reports of its neglect reached Napoleon III who, from 1854, negotiated with the British Government for its transfer to France.

In 1858 Longwood House and The Valley of the Tomb were handed over to the French State, then headed by Napoleon's nephew, Napoleon III. The French Government paid £7,100 for the properties and a condition of the transfer was that the French Government should appoint a representative responsible for their upkeep. From that date onwards a French Honorary Consul has resided on the Island. The original Briars bungalow was destroyed by termites and demolished. Much of the old Longwood House has been replaced over the years, including the floor boards built over earth and cattle dung!

Napoleon and Betsy

The story of Napoleon and Betsy Balcombe is an unusual and fascinating tale. A fallen Emperor who once controlled most of Europe makes friends with an impudent, pretty and spirited young English girl, just about the celebrate her thirteenth birthday. Betsy — later to become Elizabeth Abell

— produced a book full of interest, but because she was writing many years after the events, her book wanders backwards and forward chronologically, and as others have observed, some historical 'facts' are incorrect; but notwithstanding this, the general tenor of the relationship between this young girl and Napoleon is beyond question, and it was of an unusual and extremely friendly nature. Napoleon's fall from an unprecedented position of power to humiliating confinement must have been an impossible burden to have lived with and yet despite this — or possibly because of it — Napoleon befriended this child and held genuine affection for her. Despite the naïvety, the warmth of the friendship between the ex-Emperor and little 'Mees' Balcombe shines through, and her text is well-worth bringing to a new readership in this illustrated edition. In her book Betsy says that Napoleon was at the Briars for three months, but in actual fact it was hardly more than eight weeks, but more to the point, the family were very close to the community at Longwood, some two miles further up hill and inland, and visited weekly, sometimes more often. It was here, as Betsy matured and grew more responsible, that the friendship developed, to the extent that she assisted Napoleon with his attempts at English. She was daring as well as impudent and with an irrepressible sense of humour she unlocked the inner child in Napoleon that led to the famous friendship. He found her boldness amusing and occasionally alarming. It must have been a welcome diversion from his darker thoughts.

William Balcombe was a distinctive figure on the island, first in 1805 as a trader in Jamestown (initially in partnership with William John Burchell, the distinguished botanist) and then in 1807 he was appointed Superintendent of Public Sales for the Honourable English East India Company. By a stroke of extraordinary fortune he played host to Napoleon Bonaparte for eight weeks at the Briars, while Longwood was being made ready. In December 1815 Balcombe became purveyor to the French entourage at Longwood, a role which gave him unprecedented access and which continued until his departure from the island in March 1818. He left ostensibly because of his wife's ill health but under suspicion of being too partisan with the French. Later in the year Governor Hudson Lowe intercepted correspondence which he claimed as evidence of this, and Balcombe was not welcome to return to the island.

In the book Betsy dresses this episode up — as might have been expected: *In consequence of my mother's health declining, from the enfeebling effects of the too warm climate of St Helena, she was ordered by her medical adviser to try a voyage to England, as the only means of restoring her shattered constitution. The Winchelsea store-ship having arrived from China, my father took our passage on board, obtaining first, from Sir Hudson Lowe, six months' leave of absence from his duties as purveyor to Napoleon and his suite, etc.*

Betsy's book is undoubtedly sincere and genuine, even if her memory has played tricks on occasions. There can be little doubt that something special existed between her and one of the most able and famous men in history.

A sketch taken on HMS *Bellerophon* by Colonel Planat.

APPENDIX TO THE INTRODUCTION

Napoleon's Capture

To put Napoleon's presence on St Helena into some historical perspective, some short background may be helpful. After a series of defeats Napoleon was forced into exile on the island of Elba. He signed his abdication at Fontainbleau on 6 April 1814. He escaped from Elba with much support eleven months later and by 20 March 1815 he reached Paris, thus beginning the final reign of 100 days. Following his escape after Waterloo, 18 June 1815, Napoleon and his immediate entourage made their way via Paris to the area of Rochefort, and embarked on a French frigate. The British were blockading the coast and there was little opportunity for escape. Napoleon wished to get to the United States, but it was not to be. The following detailed account is from *The Surrender of Napoleon: being the narrative of the surrender of Buonaparte, and of his residence on board H.M.S. Bellerophon, with a detail of the principal events that occurred in that ship between the 24th of May and the 8th August 1815*. The author of this was Napoleon's captor, Rear Admiral Sir Frederick Lewis Maitland.

Order from Rear Admiral Henry Hotham to Captain Maitland HMS *Bellerophon*, dated *Superb* Quiberon Bay, 8 July 1815:

The Lords Commissioners of the Admiralty having every reason to believe that Napoleon Buonaparte meditates his escape, with his family, from France to America, you are hereby required and directed, in pursuance of orders from their Lordships, signified to me by Admiral the Right Honourable Viscount Keith, to keep the most vigilant look-out for the purpose of intercepting him; and to make the strictest search of any vessel you may fall in with; and if you should be so fortunate as to intercept him, you are to transfer him and his family to the ship you command, and keeping him in careful custody, return to the nearest port in England (going into Torbay in preference to Plymouth) with all possible expedition; and on your arrival you are not to permit any communication whatever with the shore, except as herein after directed; and you will be held responsible for keeping the whole transaction a profound secret, until you receive their Lordship's further orders.

In case you should arrive at a port where there is a flag-officer, you are to send to acquaint him with the circumstances, strictly charging the officer sent on shore with your letter, not to divulge its contents: and if there should be no flag-officer at the port where you arrive, you are to send one letter express to the Secretary of the Admiralty, and another to Admiral Lord Keith, with strict injunctions of secrecy to each officer who may be the bearer of them.

Messrs Savary and Las Cases, who came on board, from the schooner above mentioned, at seven o'clock on the 10th of July presented the following letter to me.

Translation

Sir

The Emperor Napoleon having abdicated the throne of France, and chosen the United states of America as a retreat, is, with his suite, at present embarked on board the two frigates which are in this port, for the purpose of proceeding to his destination. He expects a passport from the British government, which has been promised to him, and which induces me to send the present flag of truce, to demand of you, Sir, if you have any knowledge of the above mentioned passport, or if you think it is the intention of the British Government to throw any impediment in the way of our voyage to the United States.

I shall feel much obliged by your giving me any information you may possess on the subject. I have directed the bearers of this letter to present to you my thanks, and to apologise for the trouble it may cause.

I have the honour to be,

Your Excellency's most obedient,
Grand Marschal Count Bertrand

The bearers of the letter had instructions to demand of me, whether I would prevent Buonaparte from proceeding in a neutral vessel, provided I could not permit the frigates to pass with him on board. Having received, in my orders, the strictest injunctions to secrecy, and feeling that the force on the coast, at my disposal, was insufficient to guard the different ports and passages from which an escape might be effected, particularly should the plan be adopted of putting to sea in a small vessel; I wrote the following reply to the above communication; hoping, by that means, to induce Napoleon to remain for the Admiral's answer, which would give time for the arrival of reinforcements.

H.M.S. Bellerophon off Rochefort, July 10th 1815.

Sir,

I have to acknowledge the receipt of your letter of yesterday's date, addressed to the Admiral commanding the English cruisers before Rochefort, acquainting me that the Emperor, having abdicated the throne of France, and chosen the United States of America as an asylum, is now embarked on board the frigates, to proceed for that destination, and awaits a passport from the English Government; and requesting to know if I have any knowledge of such passport; or if I think it is the intention of the English Government to prevent the Emperor's voyage.

In reply, I have to acquaint you, that I cannot say what the intentions of my Government may be; but, the two countries being at present in a state of war, it is impossible for me to permit any ship of war to put to sea from the port of Rochefort.

As to the proposal made by the Duc de Rovigo and Count Las Cases, of allowing the Emperor to proceed in a merchant vessel; it is out of my power, – without the sanction of my commanding officer, Sir Henry Hotham, who is at present in Quiberon bay, and to whom I have forwarded your despatch, – to allow any vessel, under whatever flag she may be, to pass with a personage of such consequence. I have the honour to be.
Sir,

> *Your very humble servant,*
> > *Captain Fred. L, Maitland,*
> > > *Captain of HMS Bellerophon*

The Duke of Rovigo and Count Las Cases remained on board between two and three hours, during which time I had a great deal of conversation with them, on the state of affairs in France; in which they did all they could to impress me with the idea that Buonaparte was not reduced to the necessity of quitting Europe; but that, in doing so, he was actuated solely by motives of humanity; being unwilling, they said, that any further effusion of blood should take place on his account.

They declared also, that his party was still very formidable in the centre and south of France, and that, if he chose to protract the war, he might still give a great deal of trouble; and that, although his ultimate success might not be probable, there was still a possibility of fortune turning in his favour, and therefore they argued it was in the interest of England to allow him to proceed to America.

To all this I could give little or no reply, being quite ignorant of what had occurred in France, further than the decisive victory obtained by the Duke of Wellington at Waterloo. During the time the Frenchmen were with me, I received some French newspapers from Sir Henry Hotham; but my time was so fully occupied in writing to him. And in discussions with my visitors, that it was not in my power to read them; I therefore drew them back to the subject that occasioned their visit, and said *"Supposing the British Government should be induced to grant a passport for Buonaparte's going to America, what pledge could he give that he would not return, and put England, as well as all Europe, to the same expense of blood and treasure that has just been incurred?"*

General Savary made the following reply:

"When the Emperor first abdicated the throne of France, his removal was brought about by a faction, at the head of which was Talleyrand, and the sense of the nation was not consulted: but in the present instance he has voluntarily resigned the power. The influence he once had over the French people is past; a very considerable change has taken place in their sentiments towards him since he went to Elba; and he could never again regain the power he had over their minds: therefore he would prefer retiring into obscurity, where he might end his days in peace and tranquillity; and where he solicited to ascend the throne again, he would decline it." *"If that is the case"*, I said *"why not ask an asylum in England?"* he answered, *"There are many reasons for his not wishing to reside in England: the climate is too damp and cold; it is too near France; he would be, as it were, in the centre of every change and revolution that might take place there, and would be subject to suspicion; he has been accustomed to consider the English as his most inveterate enemies, and they have been induced to look upon him as a monster, without one of the virtues of a human being."*

This conversation took place while I was writing my despatches to Sir Henry Hotham; and the Frenchmen were walking in the cabin, frequently interrupting me, to enforce their statement of Buonaparte's situation being by no means so desperate as might be supposed; from which I took the liberty of drawing a conclusion directly opposite to the one they were desirous of impressing on my mind. Captain Knight, of *Falmouth*, who carried my despatches to the Admiral, was present during the whole of this conversation, but did not join in it.

This was the first certain information I had received of Buonaparte's position since the battle of Waterloo.

Tuesday, the 11th. [July] About noon, a small boat came off from the Island of Oleron, to where the ship was at anchor in Basque Roads, rowed by four men, in which sat two respectable-looking countrymen, who asked for the Captain; and upon my being pointed out to them, requested to speak to me in private. When shown into the cabin, where I went accompanied by Captain Gambier, of the *Myrmidon*, they acquainted me, that a message had been sent from Isle d'Aix, early that morning, for a man who was considered the best pilot on the island for the Mamusson passage, being the only person that had ever taken a frigate through; that a large sum of money had been offered to him to pilot a vessel to sea from that passage, and that it certainly was Buonaparte's intention to escape from thence; either in the corvette, which had moved down some days before, or in a Danish brig, which was then lying at anchor near the entrance.

On receiving this information, I immediately got under weigh, and though the flood-tide had just made in, beat the ships out of the Pertuis d'Antioche before it was dark, when I sent the *Myrmidon* off the Mamusson, with orders to anchor close in with the entrance, when the weather would admit of it; while I remained with the *Bellerophon* and *Slaney*, which rejoined me that evening, under weigh between the light-houses.

On the 12th of July, the *Cyrus* being seen in the offing, I ordered her by telegraph to take a position close in with the Baleine light-house, and to examine strictly every vessel that might attempt to put to sea from the Pertuis de Breton, as Buonaparte was on the spot, endeavouring to escape to America. The same evening, the white flag made its appearance for the first time on the towers of Rochelle; on seeing which, I felt it my duty to run into Basque Roads, accompanied by the *Slaney*; and having anchored, I hoisted the Bourbon colours at the main-top-gallant mast-head, and fired a royal salute.

During the whole of this afternoon, however, two tri-coloured flags were kept flying in Rochelle; and before sun-set all the white flags were struck and every where replaced by those of Buonaparte. On the 13th July, nothing of importance occurred, except the white flag being once more hoisted all over Rochelle, as well as on the Isle of Oleron, to the entire exclusion of the tri-coloured ensign.

We could plainly perceive, that the frigates, from whom we were distant about three miles, were perfectly ready to put to sea, should an opportunity offer; having their sterns covered with vegetables, their top-gallant yards across, studding sail gear rove, and numerous boats passing between them and the island the whole day:- all indications, well known to professional men, of preparing for sea.

The ships under my command were accordingly kept with slip buoys on their cables, and, as soon as it was dark, the top-sail and top-gallant yards were swayed to the mast-heads, the sails stopt with rope yarns, and every thing kept ready to make sail at a moment's warning. Guard-boats were also kept rowing all night, as near the frigates as they could venture, having signals established to show in the enemy getting under sail.

On the 14th of July, at day-break, the officer of the watch informed me, that the *Mouche* was standing out from the Isle d'Aix, bearing a flag of truce, which I ordered to be accepted.

Here it is necessary to mention, that the British flag of truce, being a white flag at the fore-top-gallant mast-head, which was also hoisted as a matter of course when Buonaparte was received on board, has by some persons been construed as the Bourbon flag, and thence into an intentional insult to him. It never was my intention, nor do I believe it could have been that of any British officer, to treat with insult any fallen enemy, much less one who had shown such confidence as to throw himself on the protection of his former foe.

When the schooner, the *Mouche*, reached the ship, Count Las Cases came on board, attended by General Count Lallemand.

This meeting was highly interesting to me, as Lallemand had been a prisoner for three weeks in the *Camelion* under my command in Egypt, with Junot, whose Aid-de-Camp he then was; and General Savary, who accompanied Count Las Cases in his first visit to the *Bellerophon*, had lived nearly as long at Sir Sydney Smith's table with me, at the Turkish camp at El Arish, when the convention, which takes its name from that place, was under discussion, being Aid-de-Camp to General Desaix, who negotiated on the part of the French.

On their coming on board, I made the signal for the captain of the *Slaney*, being desirous of having a witness to any conversation that might pass, as our communications were chiefly verbal: he arrived while we were at breakfast. When Count Las Cases came on the quarter-deck, he informed me that he was sent off to learn whether I had received a answer from the Admiral to the letter he had brought off on the 10th instant. I told him I had not, but, in consequence of the despatch which I had forwarded to him, I had not a doubt he would immediately repair here in person, and I was hourly in expectation of seeing him, adding, "*If that was the only reason you had for sending off a flag of truce, it was quite unnecessary, as I informed you, when last here, that the Admiral's answer, when it arrived, should be forwarded to the frigates by one of the Bellerophon's boats; and I did not approve of frequent communications with an enemy by means of flags of truce*" I then went into the cabin and ordered breakfast, to prevent further disussion until the arrival of Captain Sartorius.

When breakfast was over, we retired to the after cabin. Count Las Cases then said, "*The Emperor is so anxious to spare the further effusion of human blood, that he will proceed to America in any way the British Government chooses to sanction, either in a French ship of war, a vessel armed en flute, a merchant vessel, or even in a British ship of war.*" To this I answered, "*I have no authority to agree to any arrangement of that sort, nor do I believe my Government would consent to it; but I think I may venture to receive him into this ship, and convey him to England: if, however,* "I added," *he adopts that plan, I cannot enter into any promise, as to the reception he may meet with, as even in the case I have mentioned, I shall be acting on my own responsibility , and cannot be sure that it would meet with the approbation of the British Government.*"

There was a great deal of conversation on this subject, in the course Lucien Buonaparte's name was mentioned, and the manner in which he had lived in England alluded to; but I invariably assured Las Cases most explicitly, that I had no authority to make conditions of any sort, as to Napoleon's reception in England.

In fact I could not have done otherwise as I had no instructions for my guidance, and was, of course, in total ignorance of the intentions of His Majesty's ministers as to his future disposal.

One of the last observations Las Cases made before quitting the ship was, "*Under all circumstances, I have little doubt that you will see the Emperor on board the Bellerophon;*" and, in fact, Buonaparte must have determined on that step before Las Cases came on board, as his letter to His Royal Highness the Prince Regent is dated the 13th of July, the day before this conversation.

During the above-mentioned conversation, I asked Las Cases where Buonaparte then was? He replied, "*At Rochefort; I left him there yesterday evening*". General Lallemand then said, "*The Emperor lives at the Hotel in the Grand Palace, and is now so popular there, that the inhabitants assemble every evening in front of the house, for the purpose of seeing him,*" and crying "*Vive L'Empereur!*" I then asked how long it would take to go there: Las Cases answered, "*As the tide will be against us, it will require five or six hours.*"

Why these false statements were made, I cannot pretend to say; but it is very certain that Buonaparte never quitted the frigates or Isle d'Aix, after his arrival there on the 3rd of July.

General Lallemand took occasion to ask me if I thought there would be any risk of the people, who might accompany Buonaparte, being given up to the Government of France: I replied, *"Certainly not; the British Government never could think of doing so, under the circumstances contemplated in the present arrangement."*

They left me about half-past nine A.M. In the course of the day, I was joined by the *Myrmidon*, Captain Gambier, who had been sent to me by Captain Green, of the *Daphne*, with a letter he had received from Captain Aylmer, of *Pactolus*, in the Gironde, bringing information that it was the intention of Buonaparte to escape from Rochefort in a Danish sloop, concealed in a cask stowed in the ballast, with tubes so constructed as to convey air for his breathing.

I afterwards inquired of General Savary, if there had been any foundation for such a report; when he informed me that the plan had been thought of, and the vessel in some measure prepared; but it was considered too hazardous; for had we detained the vessel for a day or two, he would have been obliged to make his situation known, and thereby forfeited all claims to the good treatment he hoped to ensure by a voluntary surrender.

The two Captains dined with me, and afterwards went on board the *Myrmidon*, to take up position to the north-east of the *Bellerophon*, to prevent vessels from passing close inshore, and thus to render the blockade of the port more complete.

Soon after they left me, a barge was perceived rowing off from the frigates towards the *Bellerophon* with a flag-of-truce up; on which I recalled Captains Sartorius and Gambier, by signal, that they might be present at any communication that was made. The boat got along-side about seven P.M. and brought Count Las Cases, accompanied by General Baron Gourgaud, one of Buonaparte's Aid-de-Camps.

On their coming on deck, I immediately addressed Las Cases, saying, *"It is impossible you could have been at Rochefort, and returned, since you left me this morning."* He replied, *"No; it was not necessary; I found the Emperor at Isle d'Aix, on my arrival there."* He then told me, he was charged with a letter from General Bertrand. We walked into the cabin, when he delivered it to me; it was as follows:-

Translation

Sir,

Count Las Cases has reported to the Emperor the conversation which he had with you this morning. His Majesty will proceed on board your ship with the ebb tide to-morrow morning, between four and five o'clock.

I send the Count Las Cases, Counsellor of State, doing the duty of Marchel de Logis, with the list of persons composing His majesty's suite. If the Admiral, in consequence of the despatch you forwarded to him, should send the passport for the United States therein demanded, His Majesty will be happy to repair to America; but should the passport be withheld, he will willingly proceed to England, as a private individual, there to enjoy the protection of the laws of your country.

His Majesty has despatched Major-General Baron Gourgaud to the Prince Regent with a letter, a copy of which I have the honour to enclose, requesting that you will forward it to such one of the ministers as you may think it necessary to send that general officer, that he may have the honour of delivering the letter with which he is charged to the Prince Regent.

    I have the honour to be,

        Sir, Your humble servant,

            Count Bertrand [list of those who comprised the suite]

Enclosed was likewise a copy of the well-known letter addressed by Buonaparte to His Royal Highness the Prince Regent.

Translation

Rochefort, July 13th, 1815.

Your Royal Highness,

A victim to the factions which distract my country, and to the enmity of the greatest powers of Europe, I have terminated my political career, and I come, like Themistocles, to throw myself upon the hospitality of the British people.

I put myself under the protection of their laws; which I claim from your Royal Highness, as the most powerful, the most constant, and the most generous of my enemies.

    Napoleon.

On reading the above, I told Monsieur Las Cases that I would receive Buonaparte on board, and immediately forward General Gourgaud to England by the *Slaney*, along with my despatches to the Admiralty; but that he would not be allowed to land until permission was received from London, or the sanction of the Admiral at the port he might arrive obtained.

I assured him, however, that the copy of the letter with which he was charged would be forwarded without loss of time, and presented by the Ministers to His Royal highness, Count Las Cases then asked for paper, that he might communicate by letter to Bertrand my acquiescence in the proposal he had brought, for my receiving, and conveying to England, Buonaparte and his suite.

When General Gourgaud was about to write the letter, to prevent any future misunderstanding, I said, *"Monsieur Las Cases, you will recollect that I am not authorised to stipulate as to the reception of Buonaparte in England, but that he must consider himself entirely at the disposal of His Royal Highness the Prince Regent."* He answered, *"I am perfectly aware of that, and have already acquainted the Emperor with what you said on that subject".*

It might, perhaps, have been better if this declaration had been given in an official written form; and could I have foreseen the discussions which afterwards took place, and which will appear in the sequel, I undoubtedly should have done so; but as I repeatedly made it in the presence of witnesses, it did not occur to me as being necessary; and how could a stronger proof be adduced, that no stipulations were agreed to respecting the reception of Buonaparte in England, than the fact of their not being in writing? Which certainly would have been the case had any favourable terms been demanded on the part of Monsieur Las Cases, and agreed to by me.

The French boat was soon after despatched with the letter from Bertrand, in charge of a French naval officer, who had attended Las Cases on board; and as soon as I had finished the following despatch to the Secretary of the Admiralty, I sent Captain Sartorious, of the *Slaney*, to England, accompanied by General Gourgaud.

Extract of a letter from Captain Maitland, of His Majesty's ship *Bellerophon*, addressed to the Secretary of the Admiralty, dated in Basque Roads, 14th July, 1815.

For the information of the Lords Commissioners of the Admiralty,

I have to acquaint you that the Count Las Cases and General Lallemand this day came on board His Majesty's ship under my command, with a proposal from Count Bertrand for me to receive on board Napoleon Buonaparte, for the purpose of throwing himself on the generosity of the Prince Regent.

Conceiving myself authorised by their Lordships' secret order, I have accede to the proposal, and he is embark on board this ship tomorrow morning.

That no misunderstanding should arise, I have explicitly and clearly explained to Count Las Cases, that I have no authority whatever for granting terms of any sort, but that all I can do is to carry him and his suite to England, to be received in such a manner as his Royal Highness may deem expedient.

At Napoleon Buonaparte's request, and that their Lordships may be in possession of the transaction at as early a period as possible, I despatch the *Slaney* (with General Gourgaud, his Aid de Camp), directing Captain Sartorious to put into the nearest port, and forward this letter by his first lieutenant, and shall in compliance with their Lordships' orders proceed to Torbay, to await such directions as the Admiralty shall think proper to give. Enclosed, I transmit a copy of the letter with which General Gourgaud is charged, to his Royal Highness the Prince Regent, and request that you will acquaint their Lordships, that the General informs me, he is entrusted with further particulars, which he is anxious to communicate to his Royal Highness.

When these gentlemen had left the ship, as well as the *Slaney's* barge, I said to Monsieur Las Cases, I propose dividing the after-cabin in two, that the ladies may have the use of part of it. *"If you allow me to give an opinion,"* said he, *"the Emperor will be better pleased to have the whole after cabin to himself, as he is fond of walking about, and will by that means be able to take more exercise."* I answered, *"As it is my wish to treat him with every possible consideration while he is on board the ship I command, I shall make any arrangement you think will be most agreeable to him."*

This is the only conversation that ever passed on the subject of the cabin; and I am the more particular in stating it, as Buonaparte has been described, in some public Journals, as having taken possession of it in the most brutal way, saying, *"Tout ou rien pour moi:"* — All or nothing for me.

I here therefore, once for all, beg to state most distinctly, that, from the time of his coming on board my ship, to the period of his quitting her, his conduct was invariably that of a gentleman; and in no one instance do I recollect him to have made use of a rude expression, or to have been guilty of ill-breeding.

As the ship had for some time been kept clear for action, with all the bulkheads down, it became necessary to prepare for the reception of so many guests, by putting the cabins up again: inconsequence of making the requisite arrangements, it was past one o'clock in the morning before I could get to bed.

About ten at night, the officer of the watch informed me that a boat from the shore had asked permission to come alongside. A man being allowed to come on board from her; "I am sent off from Rochelle," said he, "to inform you that Buonaparte this morning passed that town in a chassee-marée, with another in company, for the purpose of escaping to sea by the Pertuis de Breton: he is now in that passage, and means to set sail this night." I told him, "that I doubted his information, having at that moment one of his attendants on board, who had come with a proposal for me to receive him into the ship.

I then asked him how he came by his intelligence? he answered, "The vessels passed close to a boat I was in; and I saw a man wrapped up in a sailor's great coat, whom one of the people with me asserted to be him: for my part, I am not aquainted with his appearance, never having seen him; but when the owner of the vessels attempted to go on board one of them, he was kept off, and told that they would be required for two or three days, when they would be restored with ample payment."

He told his story so circumstantially, and with such confidence, that I feared there must be just grounds for what he stated; and the anxiety of my situation can easily be conceived, when it is recollected that I had sent off a ship for England with despatches, announcing the intention of Buonaparte to embark the following morning in the *Bellerophon*.

After a little consideration, I determined to inform Las Cases abruptly of the intelligence I had received, and endeavour to judge by the effect it had on his countenance, whether there was any truth in the report or not. I accordingly went into the cabin and did so; he seemed perfectly calm and collected, saying, "pray at what hour does your informant state the Emperor to have passed Rochelle?" "At ten A.M." "Then I can safely assert, on my honour, that he was not in either of these vessels. I left him at half-past five this evening, when it was his full intention to come on board this ship tomorrow morning; what he may have done since that hour, I cannot be responsible for." I answered, "As you give your word of honour that Buonaparte had not left the Isle d'Aix when you quitted it, I shall trust to what you say, and take no steps in consequence of the information that has been brought to me, but concluded it has originated in some mistake."

About three in the morning, the officer of the watch awoke me, and said that another boat wished to come alongside. I rose and found that she brought the same intelligence from another quarter; and they both eventually proved correct, to a certain extent; for two chasee-marées, as I was afterwards informed, had been prepared, manned, and officered from the frigates, to be used as a last resource to attempt an escape in, in the event of Las Cases' mission to the *Bellerophon* not being successful; and they had actually passed Rochelle, in their way to Pointeau d'Aguillon, at the hour specified, and were there to wait his joining them should it prove necessary.

After I had determined to abide by Las Cases' evening, assurance, that Buonaparte had not quitted Isle d'Aix, I enquired of the person who brought off the information in the evening "What was the state of Rochelle, and whether

I might with safety send a boat there to purchase refreshments?" as the white flag was then hoisted all over the town; he said, "he would not recommend it, as, though the towns people were well inclined towards the Bourbon family, the garrison, consisting of four thousand men, were all attached to Buonaparte; but if he were once on board the ship, there would be no risk in doing so, as their fear of his meeting with bad treatment would keep the soldier in awe."

At break of day, on the 15th July, 1815, *L'Epervier* French brig of war was discovered under sail, standing out towards the ship, with a flag of truce up; and at the same time the *Superb*, bearing Henry Hotham's flag, was seen in the offing.

By half-past five the ebb-tide failed, the wind was blowing right in, and the brig, which was within a mile of us, made no further progress; whilst the *Superb* was advancing with the wind and tide in her favour. Thus situated, and being most anxious to terminate the affair I had brought so near to conclusion, previous to the Admiral's arrival, I sent off Mr Mott, the first lieutenant, in the barge, who returned soon after six o'clock, bringing Napoleon with him.

On coming on board the *Bellerophon*, he was received without any of the honours generally paid to persons of high rank; the guard was drawn out on the break of the poop, but did no present arms. His Majesty's Government had merely given directions, in the event of his being captured, for his being removed into any one of his Majesty's ships that might fall in with him; but no instructions had been given as to the light in which he was to be viewed. As it is not customary, however, on board a British ship of war, to pay any such honours before the colours are hoisted at eight o'clock in the morning, or after sunset, I made the early hour an excuse for with-holding them upon this occasion.

Buonaparte's dress was an olive-coloured great coat over a green uniform, with scarlet cape and cuffs, green lapels turned back and edged with scarlet, skirts hooked back with bugle horns embroidered in gold, plain sugar-loaf buttons and gold epaulettes; being the uniform of the Chasseur à Cheval of the Imperial Guard. He wore the star or grand cross of the Legion of Honour, and the small cross of that order; the Iron Crown; and the Union, appended to the button-hole of his left lapel. He had on a small cocked hat, with a tri-coloured cockade; plain gold-hilted sword, military boots, and white waistcoat and breeches.

The following day he appeared in shoes, with gold buckles, and silk stocking — the dress he always wore afterwards, while with me.

On leaving the *Epervier*, he was cheered by her ship's company as long as the boat was in hearing; and Mr Mott informed me that most of the officers and men had tears in their eyes.

Although the above account is highly detailed, the description of the negotiations that went on during these few days is well worth repeating.

Nine days later, 24 July 1815, in accordance with his instructions, Maitland anchored at Torbay. Two days later, 26 July 1815, HMS *Bellerophon* arrived at Plymouth Sound, but Napoleon was not allowed to leave the ship. In fact the British cabinet had already met and decided on 20 July 1815 that he would be removed to a secure exile at St Helena, a place which the Government hoped would be in-escapable, but notwithstanding that expectation, paranoia continued and there was more than one plot later reported. On 30 July, Lord Bathurst, the Secretary for War and the Colonies, set the 26 regulations for the custody of Napoleon and on 31 July 1815 a representative of Lord Bathurst met Napoleon and told him of the British Government's decision to deport him to the island of St. Helena for custody. HMS *Bellerophon* left Plymouth on 4 August and on 6 August rendezvoused with HMS *Northumberland* at which point Napoleon and his entourage were transferred. Their final comrades boarded on 7 August and on 8 August sailed under the command of Sir George Cockburn and arrived at St Helena 15 October 1815. The voyage and the diary details that accompany this are published in other Fonthill books, see the web site for detail.

A tumbler given by Napoleon to Captain Maitland, bearing the monogram 'J' for 'Josephine'.

The King of Rome, a lithograph after a painting by Sir Thomas Lawrence.

Napoléon II — Napoleon François Charles Joseph, (1811-1832), was the son of Napoleon and his second wife, Marie Louise of Austria. He was Prince Imperial, but he was also known from birth as the King of Rome which Napoleon declared was the courtesy title of the heir-apparent. When Napoleon abdicated in April 1814, he named his son Emperor, but the Allies refused to acknowledge him. Napoleon was intensely fond and proud of his son, but he never saw him after 1814.

Marie-Louise returned to Austria and in 1818 his maternal grandfather, Emperor Francis of Austria created him Duke of Reichstadt and he became know as 'Franz'. Upon the death of his stepfather, Count Neipperg, and the revelation that his mother had borne two illegitimate children to him prior to her marriage, Franz said to his friend, Prokesch von Osten, "If Josephine had been my mother, my father would not have been buried at Saint Helena, and I should not be at Vienna. My mother is kind but weak; she was not the wife my father deserved".

Napoléon II died of tuberculosis at Schönbrunn Palace in Vienna on 22 July 1832. On 15 December 1940, his remains were transferred from Vienna to the dome of Les Invalides as a gift to France by Adolf Hitler. For some time, the young prince who had briefly been an Emperor rested beside his father. Later the remains of the prince were moved to the lower church.

See page 58.

RECOLLECTIONS
OF NAPOLEON
AT ST HELENA

Lucia Elizabeth Abell

A lithograph of a sketch of the Briars made by Lucia Elizabeth Abell (Betsy Balcombe) that formed the frontispiece of her book.

PREFACE

The writer of the following pages trusts she will not be thought presumptuous in presenting them to the public. Thrown at a very early age into the society of Napoleon, and of those who composed his suite, she considers it an almost imperative duty to communicate any fact or impression, which, though uninteresting in itself, may still be worth recording as relating to him, and as serving to elucidate his character. Could these recollections of the emperor have been published without having her name appended to them, they would long ago have appeared, but feeling that the sole merit to which they could lay claim consisted in their being faithful records of him, and that if produced anonymously, there would be no guarantee for their truth; being moreover desirous to shun publicity, and unequal to the task of authorship, the undertaking has been postponed from time to time, and, perhaps, would have been delayed still longer, but for the pressure of calamitous circumstances, which compels her to hesitate no more, but, with all their imperfections on their head, to send these pages at once into the world.

The authoress may compare her feelings, as she launches her little vessel on the waters, to those of Shelley, when, having exhausted his whole stock of paper, he twisted a bank-note into the shape of a little boat, and then committing it to the stream, waited on the other side for its arrival with intense anxiety. Her shipbuilding powers, she fears, are as feeble, her materials as frail; but she has seen the little Paper Nautilus floating with impunity and confidence on the bosom of that mighty ocean, which has engulfed many a noble vessel: accepting the augury, she intrusts her tiny bark to the waves of public opinion, not with confidence, however, but with timidity and hesitation, — yet is her solicitude not altogether unenlivened by the hope that it may reach its haven, if wafted by friendly breezes and favoured by propitious skies.

The writer must crave indulgence for the frequent mention of herself during the narrative. The nature of the subject, renders this unavoidable.

Lucia Elizabeth Abell

A French plan of Longwood and its garden, 1821.

CONTENTS

The Briars from a late-nineteenth-century photograph. The main house is hidden behind trees and shrubbery, but the Pavilion is visible on the right. The heart-shaped waterfall is clearly visible, as is the steep trackway winding up the hill behind. The house was destroyed by 'white ants' and demolished some time before the Second World War.

CHAPTER I

My object in the following Memoir is to confine myself, as far as possible, to what concerns Napoleon personally. Having, however, many reminiscences, unconnected with him, of the happy days of my childhood, and feeling that they might be interesting to the public, *especially* to those who visited the island during the emperor's captivity there, I venture to insert them. A slight description of the localities connected with Napoleon will not, I trust, be considered uninteresting to my readers, and I may, perhaps, commence this slight memoir most properly, by a few remarks upon the general aspect of St Helena, and of the impression conveyed by it, on first approaching its shores.

The appearance of St Helena, on viewing it from the sea, is different from that of any land I ever saw, and is certainly but little calculated to make one fall in love with it at first sight. The rock, rising abruptly from the ocean, with its oblong shape and perpendicular sides, suggests to one's mind more the idea of a huge dark-coloured ark lying at anchor, floating on the bosom of the Atlantic, than of a land intended for the habitation and support of living beings; nor, on a nearer acquaintance, does its character become more amiable. If a stranger approach it during the night, the effect on coming on deck in the morning is most peculiar, and at first, almost alarming. From the great depth of water, ships are able to run very close in, to the land; and the eye, long accustomed to the expanse of sea and atmosphere, is suddenly startled by coming almost, as it seems, in contact with the dark threatening rock towering hundreds of feet into the air, far above the masts of the tallest vessel.

I was quite a child at the time of my first visit, and my terrors were increased by being told that the giant-snouted crag, which bore some resemblance to the head of a negro, when the breakfast bell struck, would devour me first, and afterwards the rest of the passengers and crew. I rushed instantly below, and hiding my face on my mother's lap, tremblingly announced our fate. It was not without much difficulty that she succeeded in soothing my terrors, by assurances of safety and protection. But I did not venture from under her wing until the dreaded "eight bells" had sounded, and the appearance of breakfast announced better things in store for us. I was told that even the mighty heart of Napoleon sank within him, when he first surveyed his future home; and as the *Northumberland* glided to her anchorage, revealing the galleries of the batteries on either side, bristling with cannon, and frowning heavily upon him; the despairing inscription which the beautiful language of his infancy had rendered familiar to him, seemed to have been inscribed on the gloomy rock:—

"Lasciate ogni speranza voi ch'entrate.'

On rounding Munden's battery, James Town breaks upon the view. It is singular and striking, and quite in harmony with the rest of the peculiar scenery of St Helena. The houses are all built at the bottom of a wide ravine, which looks as if it had been caused by some great convulsion of nature, or as if the rock, tired of its solitary life and isolated situation in the midst of the Atlantic, had given a great yawn, and had then been unable to close its mouth again. The buildings are confined entirely to the bottom of this cleft or chasm, as its sides are too precipitous to allow of houses being built on them. The position of the town renders it sufficiently hot in summer. The cool sea breeze, so delicious in all tropical climates, is almost excluded by the situation of the valley, as the inhabitants call James Town, and for nine months in the year the heat is almost unendurable.

We were fortunate enough to reside out of town, my father possessing a beautiful little cottage called the Briars, about a mile and a quarter from the valley; a spot meriting a slight description, both from its intrinsic beauty, and from having been the residence of Napoleon during the first three months of his exile in St Helena.

The way to the Briars, winds out of the town by roads cut in the side of the mountain. I cannot say I saw much of this road or the surrounding scenery, on my first journey to our distant abode; I was on that occasion put into a basket, and carried on a negro's head, who trudged away with me very merrily, singing some joyous air. Occasionally he put me down to rest, and, grinning from ear to ear, asked me if I felt comfortable in my little nest. I was rather frightened, as this was the first time I had seen a black man; but I soon reconciled myself to him, and we became great friends. He told me, he generally carried vegetables into the valley, and appeared highly honoured, and proud that a living burden should have been confided to his care. I was soon deposited in safety at the door of the Briars, and bade adieu to my sable bearer, who went away quite delighted with some little present my father gave him for making himself so amiable to me.

Our cottage was built in the style of the bungalows in India; it was very low, the rooms being chiefly on one floor, and, had it not been for its situation, would not have been thought so pretty; but surrounded, as this verdant spot was, by barren mountains, it looked a perfect little paradise — an Eden blooming in the midst of desolation. A beautiful avenue of banyan trees led up to it, and either side was flanked by evergreen and gigantic lacos, interspersed with pomegranate and myrtle, and a profusion of large white roses, much resembling our sweetbriar, from which, indeed, the place derived its name. A walk, shaded by pomegranate trees, thirty or forty feet in height, conducted to the garden.

I must plead the same excuse for devoting a few lines to the garden that I have to the cottage, for it was lovely in itself, and the favourite retreat of the emperor during his sojourn with us. It would require the pen of a Scott, or the pencil of a Claude, to do anything like justice to its beauty. I often wander in my dreams through its myrtle groves, and the orange trees, with their bright green leaves, delicious blossoms, and golden fruit, seem again before me, as they were in my blessed days of childhood. Every description of tropical fruit flourished here luxuriantly; various species of vine, citron, orange, fig, shadoc, guava, mango — all in endless profusion.

The produce of this garden alone, which the family could not consume, brought annually from £500 to £600. Nature, as if jealous of the beauty of this enchanting spot, had surrounded it on every side with impenetrable barriers. On the east, to speak geographically, it was bounded by a precipice, so steep as to render all approach impracticable. The dark frowning mountain, called Peak Hill, rendered it inaccessible from the south; to the westward it was protected by a cataract, in itself a most picturesque and striking object. I forget its height, but its roar was very imposing to me, and the volume of water must have been considerable. In that hot climate it was a delightful next-door neighbour; in the most sultry day one could hardly feel the heat oppressive, when gazing on its cool and sparkling waters. On the side nearest the cottage the defences of the garden were completed by an aloe and prickly pear hedge, through which no living thing could penetrate. The garden at the Briars, like the bright dreams and hopes of my own early youth, is now withered and destroyed: it was sold to the East India Company, by whom it was dug up, and planted with mulberry trees, which speedily became "food for worms," if I may be guilty of a conceit on — to me — melancholy subject. I believe the intended speculation proved unsuccessful.

CHAPTER II

We had been living for years in this romantic and secluded glen, when our little "isle was suddenly *frighted from its propriety*" by hearing that Napoleon Bonaparte was to be confined as a prisoner of state. It was in October, 1815, that this news first burst upon us. We heard one morning an alarm gun fired from Ladder Hill, which was the signal that a vessel was in sight, off the island. The same evening, two naval officers arrived at the Briars, one of whom was announced as Captain D., commanding the *Icarus* man-of-war.[1] He requested to see my father, having intelligence of importance to communicate to him. On being conducted to him, he informed him that Napoleon Bonaparte was on board the *Northumberland*, under the command of Sir George Cockburn, and within a few days' sail of the island. The news of his, escape from Elba, and the subsequent eventful campaign had, of course, not reached us, and I remember well how amazed and incredulous they all seemed to be at the information. Captain D. was obliged more than once to assure them of the correctness of his statement. My own feeling at the intelligence was excessive terror, and an undefined conviction that something awful would happen to us all, though of what nature I hardly knew. I glanced eagerly at my father, and seeing his countenance calm, I became more composed, but still I listened to every word of Captain D's detail as if my fate depended on what he was telling us. The earliest idea I had of Napoleon was that of a huge ogre or giant, with one large flaming red eye in the middle of his forehead, and long teeth protruding from his mouth, with which he tore to pieces and devoured naughty little girls, especially those who did not know their lessons. I had rather grown out of this first opinion of Napoleon; but, if less childish, my terror of him was still hardly diminished. The name of Bonaparte was still associated, in my mind, with everything that was bad and horrible. I had heard the most atrocious crimes imputed to him; and if I had learned to consider him as a human being, I yet still believed him to be the worst that had ever existed. Nor was I singular in these feelings; they were participated by many much older and wiser than myself; I might say, perhaps, by a majority of the English nation. Most of the newspapers of the day described him as a demon; and all those of his own country who lived in England were of course his bitter enemies; and from these two sources alone we formed our opinion of him. It was not, therefore, without uneasiness, that I saw my father depart, a day or two afterwards, to go on board the vessel which had just cast anchor in the bay. The fleet consisted of the *Northumberland*, commanded by Sir George Cockburn,[2] to whose care Napoleon had been confided; the *Havannah*, Captain Hamilton,[3] and several other men-of-war, together with transports containing the 53rd regiment. We remained many hours in great anxiety; at last my father returned from his visit in safety, and we rushed out to question him as to what had occurred.

"Well, papa, have you seen him?" we exclaimed, for we thought of no one but Napoleon. He told us he had not seen the emperor, but had paid his respects to Sir George Cockburn, and had been introduced to Madame Bertrand, Madame Montholon, and the rest of Napoleon's suite. He added that General Bonaparte would land in the evening and was to remain for the present at the house of a Mr Porteus, until Longwood, which was intended for his ultimate residence, Should be ready for him. We were so eager to see the illustrious exile that we determined to go in the evening to the valley to witness his disembarkation. It was nearly dark when we arrived at the landing place, and shortly after, a boat from the *Northumberland* approached, and we saw a figure step from it on the shore, which we were told was the emperor, but it war too dark to distinguish his features. He walked up the lines between the Admiral and General Bertrand, and enveloped as he was in his surtout,[4] I could see little, but the occasional gleam of a diamond star, which he wore on his heart. The whole population of St Helena had crowded to behold him, and one could hardly have believed that it contained so many inhabitants. The pressure became so great that it was with difficulty way could he made for him, and the sentries were at last ordered to stand with fixed bayonets at the entrance from the lines to the town, to prevent the multitude from pouring in. Napoleon was excessively provoked at the eagerness of the crowd to get a peep at him, more particularly as he was received in silence though with respect. I heard him afterwards say how much he had been annoyed at being followed and stared at "comme une bête feroçe."

We returned to the Briars that night to talk and dream of Napoleon.

CHAPTER III

The next morning, we observed a large cavalcade moving along the path which wound round the mountain, at the base of which our dear little cottage was lying, almost hidden in its nest of leaves. The effect of the party was very picturesque. It consisted of five horsemen, and we watched them with great interest, as, following the windings of the road, they now gleamed in the sun's rays, and were thrown into brilliant relief by the dark background behind, and then disappearing, we gazed earnestly until, from some turn in the road, they flashed again upon us. Sometimes we only saw a single white plume, or the glitter of a weapon in the sun. To my already excited fancy, it suggested the idea of an enormous serpent with burnished scales, occasionally showing himself as he crawled to our little abode.

We were still doubtful whether Napoleon were of the party. We had already learnt to look for the grey surtout and small cocked hat, but no figure in that dress could be distinguished, though our spy-glass was in anxious requisition. Everyone thought he would be best able to discover him. At last, one of the party exclaimed, "I see a figure with a small cocked hat, but no great coat;" and then we were at last certain that it was the emperor. We concluded he was on his way to Longwood, to look at his future residence.

About two o'clock on that day, Mr O'Meara, and Dr Warden called on us, and were overwhelmed with all kinds of questions about Bonaparte, his manner, appearance, etc., etc. They described him as most agreeable and pleasing, and assured us we should be delighted with him. But all their fair words were thrown away upon me; I could think of him only with fear and trembling. When leaving us, they again repeated that our opinion of Napoleon would entirely change when we had once seen and conversed with him.

At four o'clock in the evening, the same horsemen whom we had seen in the morning, again appeared on their return from Longwood. As soon as they reached the head of the narrow pass which led down to the Briars, they halted, and after apparently a short deliberation, with terror I saw them begin to descend the mountain and approach our cottage. I recollect feeling so dreadfully frightened, that I wished to run and hide myself until they were gone; but mamma desired me to stay, and to remember and speak French as well as I could. I had learned that language during a visit my father had paid to England some years before, and as we had a French servant, I had not lost what I had then acquired.

The party arrived at the gate, and there being no carriage-road, they all dismounted, excepting the emperor, who was now fully visible. He retained his seat and rode up the avenue, his horse's feet cutting up the turf on our pretty lawn. Sir George Cockburn walked on one side of his horse, and General Bertrand on the other.[5] How vividly I recollect my feelings of dread mingled with admiration, as I now first looked upon him whom I had learned to fear so much. His appearance on horseback was noble and imposing. The animal he rode was a superb one; his colour Jet black; and as he proudly stepped up the avenue, arching his neck and champing his bit, I thought he looked worthy to be the bearer of him who was once the ruler of nearly the whole European world!

Napoleon's position on horseback, by adding height to his figure, supplied all that was wanting to make me think him the most majestic person I had ever seen. His dress was green, and covered with orders, and his saddle and housings were of crimson velvet richly embroidered with gold. He alighted at our house, and we all moved to the entrance to receive him. Sir George Cockburn introduced us to him.

On a nearer approach Napoleon, contrasting, as his shorter figure did, with the noble height and aristocratic bearing of Sir George Cockburn, lost something of the dignity which had so much struck me on first seeing him. He was deadly pale, and I thought his features, though cold and immovable, and somewhat stern, were exceedingly beautiful. He seated himself on one of our cottage chairs, and after scanning our little apartment with his eagle glance, he complimented mamma on the pretty situation of the Briars. When once he began to speak, his fascinating smile and kind manner removed every vestige of the fear with which I had hitherto regarded him.

While he was talking to mamma, I had an opportunity of scrutinizing his features, which I did with the keenest interest; and certainly I have never seen anyone with so remarkable and striking a physiognomy. The portraits of him, give a good general idea of his features; but his smile, and the expression of his eye, could not be transmitted to canvas, and these constituted Napoleon's chief charm. His hair was dark brown, and as fine and silky as a child's, rather too much so indeed for a man, as its very softness caused it to look thin. His teeth were even, but rather dark, and I afterwards found that this arose from his constant habit of eating liquorice, of which he always kept a supply in his waistcoat pocket.

The emperor appeared much pleased with the Briars, and expressed a wish to remain there. My father had offered Sir George Cockburn apartments at the cottage, and he immediately assured us of his willingness to resign them to General Bonaparte, as the situation appeared to please him so much; and it was arranged, much apparently to Napoleon's satisfaction, that he should be our guest until his residence at Longwood were fit to receive him.

Our family at the time of the emperor's arrival, consisted of my father, my mother, my elder sister, myself, and my two brothers, who were quite children. Napoleon determined on not going down to the town again, and wished his rooms to be got ready for him immediately. Some chairs were then brought out at his request, upon the lawn, and seating himself on one, he desired me to take another, which I did with a beating heart. He then said, "You speak French:" I replied that I did, and he asked me who had taught me. I informed him, and he put several questions to me about my studies, and more particularly concerning geography. He inquired the capitals of the different countries of Europe. "What is the capital of France?" "Paris." "Of Italy?" "Rome." "Of Russia?" "Petersburg now," I replied; "Moscow formerly." On my saying this, he turned abruptly round, and, fixing his piercing eyes full in my face, he demanded sternly Qui l'a brulé?" When I saw the expression of his eye, and heard his changed voice, all my former terror of him returned, and I was unable to utter a syllable.

I had often heard the burning of Moscow talked of, and had been present at discussions, as to whether the French or Russians were the authors of that dreadful conflagration, I therefore feared to offend him by alluding to it. He repeated the question, and I stammered, "I do not know, sir." "Oui, oui," he replied, laughing violently: "Vous savez très bien, ç'est moi qui l'a brulé." On seeing him laugh, I gained a little courage, and said, "I believe, sir, the Russians burnt it to get rid of the French." He again laughed and seemed pleased to find that I knew anything about the matter.

The arrangements made for him were necessarily most hurried; and while we were endeavouring to complete them in the way we thought most likely to contribute to his comfort, he amused himself by walking about the grounds and garden.

In the evening he came into the house; and as my father and mother spoke French with difficulty, that language being then much less studied in

England than it is at present, he addressed himself again to me, and asked me whether I liked music, adding, "You are too young to play yourself." I felt rather piqued at this, and told him I could both sing and play. He then asked me to sing, and I sang, as well as I could, the Scotch song, "Ye banks and braes." When I finished, he said it was the prettiest English air he had ever heard. I replied it was a Scottish ballad, not English; and he remarked, he thought it too pretty to be English: "their music is vile — the worst in the world." He then inquired if I knew any French songs, and among others, "Vive Henri Quatre." I said I did not. He began to hum the air, became abstracted, and, leaving his seat, marched round the room, keeping time to the song he was singing. When he had done, he asked me what I thought of it; and I told him I did not like it at all, for I could not make out the air. In fact, Napoleon's voice was most unmusical, nor do I think he had any ear for music; for neither on this occasion, nor in any of his subsequent attempts at singing, could I ever discover what tune it was he was executing. He was, nevertheless, a good judge of music, if any Englishwoman may say so, after his sweeping denunciation of our claims to that science, probably from having constantly listened to the best performers. He expressed a great dislike to French music, which, he said, was almost as had as the English, and that the Italians were the only people who could produce an opera.

A lady, a friend of ours, who frequently visited us at the Briars, was extremely fond of Italian singing, which "she loved, indeed, not wisely, but too well," for her own attempts in the bravura style were the most absurd burlesque imaginable. Napoleon, however, constantly asked her to sing, and even listened with great politeness; but when she was gone, he often desired me to imitate her singing, which I did as nearly as I could, and it seemed to amuse him. He used to shut his eyes and pretend he thought it was Mrs ——, "our departed friend," and then pay me gravely the same compliments he would have done to her.

The emperor retired for the night, shortly after my little attempt to amuse him, and thus terminated his first day at the Briars.

CHAPTER IV

It is not in my power to give a detailed account of the events of each day the emperor spent with us. I shall never cease regretting that I did not keep a journal of all that occurred, but I was too young and too thoughtless to see the advantage of doing so; besides, I trusted to a memory naturally most retentive, thinking it would enable me at any time to recall the minutest incident concerning Napoleon. In this I have deceived myself. My life has been a chequered and a melancholy one, and many of its incidents have been of a nature to absorb the mind and abstract the attention from everything but the consideration of present misery. This, continued for a length of time, has erased things from my recollection which I thought I never could have forgotten, but of which I now retain nothing but the consciousness that they took place, and the regret that I am unable to record them.

Many of the circumstances I am about to relate, however, I did write down shortly after they occurred, and the others have been kept fresh in my memory by being repeated to friends; so that the reader of my little volume may depend on the absolute truth and fidelity of my narrative, a consideration, indeed, to which I have thought it right to sacrifice many others. I do not, then, profess to give a journal of what Napoleon *daily* said and did at the Briars; but the occurrences related I have inserted as nearly as possible in the order in which they took place.

The emperor's habits, during the time he stayed with us, were very simple and regular. His usual hour for getting up was eight, and he seldom took anything but a cup of coffee until one, when he breakfasted, or rather lunched; he dined at nine, and retired about eleven to his own rooms. His manner was so unaffectedly kind and amiable, that in a few days I felt perfectly at ease in his society, and looked upon him more as a companion of my own age, than as the mighty warrior at whose name "the world grew pale." His spirits were very good, and he was at times almost boyish in his love of mirth and glee, not unmixed sometimes with a tinge of malice.

Shortly after his arrival, a little girl, Miss Legg, the daughter of a friend, came to visit us at the Briars. The poor child had heard such terrific stories of Bonaparte, that when I told her he was coming up the lawn, she clung to me in an agony of terror. Forgetting my own former fears, I was cruel enough to run out and tell Napoleon of the child's fright, begging him to come into the house. He walked up to her, and, brushing up his hair with his hand, shook his head, making horrible faces, and giving a sort of savage howl. The little girl screamed so violently, that mamma was afraid she would go into hysterics, and took her out of the room. Napoleon laughed a good deal at the idea of his being such a bugbear, and would hardly believe me when I told him that I had stood in the same dismay of him. When I made this confession, he tried to frighten me as he had poor little Miss Legg, by brushing up his hair, and distorting his features; but he looked more grotesque than horrible, and I only laughed at him. He then (as a last resource) tried the howl, but was equally unsuccessful, and seemed, I thought, a little provoked that he could not frighten me. He said the howl was Cossack, and it certainly was barbarous enough for anything.

He took a good deal of exercise at this period, and was fond of taking exploring walks in the valley and adjacent mountain. One evening he strolled out, accompanied by General Gourgaud,[6] my sister, and myself, into a meadow in which some cows were grazing. One of these, the moment she saw our party, put her head down and (I believe) her tail up, and advanced *à pas de charge* against the emperor. He made a skilful and rapid retreat, and leaping nimbly over a wall, placed this rampart between himself and the enemy. But General Gourgaud valiantly stood his around, and, drawing his sword, threw himself between his sovereign and the cow, exclaiming, "This is the second time I have saved the emperor's life." Napoleon laughed heartily when he heard the General's boast, and said, "He ought to have put himself in the position to repel cavalry." I told him the cow appeared tranquillized, and stopped the moment he disappeared, and he continued to laugh, and said, "She wished to save the English government the expense and trouble of keeping him."

The emperor, during his residence under my father's roof, occupied only one room and a marquee; the room was one my father had built for a ball-room. There was a small lawn in front, railed round, and in this railing the marquee was pitched, connected with the house by a covered way. The marquee was divided into two compartments, the inner one forming Napoleon's bedroom, and at one extremity of the external compartment there was a small tent bed, with green silk hangings, on which General Gourgaud slept. It was the bedstead used by the emperor in all his campaigns. Between the two divisions of the tent was a crown, which his devoted servants bad carved out of the turf floor, and it was so placed, that the emperor could not pass through, without placing his foot on this emblem of royal dignity.

Napoleon seemed to have no *penchant* for the pleasures of the table. He lived very simply, and cared little or nothing about what he ate. He dined at nine, and at that hour Cipriani, the *maître d'hôtel*, made his appearance, and with a profound reverence said, in a solemn tone, "Le dîner de votre Majesté est servi." He then retreated backwards, followed by Napoleon and those of his suite who were to dine with him. When he had finished, he would abruptly push away his chair from the table, and quit the dining-room, apparently glad it was over.

A few days after his arrival, he invited my sister and myself to dine with him, and began quizzing the English for their fondness for *rosbif* and plum pudding. I accused the French, in return, of living on frogs; and, running into the house, I brought him a caricature of a long, lean Frenchman, with his month open, his tongue out, and a frog on the tip of it, ready to jump down his throat: underneath was written, "A Frenchman's dinner!" He laughed at my impertinence, and pinched my ear, as he often did when he was amused, and sometimes when a little provoked at my "*espiéglerie.*"

"Le petit Las Cases," as he called Count Las Cases' son,[7] formed one of the party on that day. He was then a lad of fourteen, and the emperor was fond of quizzing me about him, and telling me I should be his wife. Nothing enraged me so much; I could not bear to be considered such a child, and particularly at that moment, for there was a ball in prospect, to which I had great hopes papa would allow me to go, and I knew that his objection would be founded on my being too young. Napoleon, seeing my annoyance, desired young Las Cases to kiss me, and he held both my hands whilst the little page saluted me. I did all in my power to escape, but in vain. The moment, however, that my hands were at liberty, I boxed le petit Las Cases' ears most thoroughly. But I determined to be revenged on Napoleon, and in descending to the cottage to play whist, an opportunity presented itself which I did not allow to escape. There was no internal communication between the part occupied by the emperor and the rest of the house, and the path leading down was very steep and very narrow. There being barely room for one person to pass at a time, Napoleon walked first, Las Cases next, then his son, and, lastly, my sister Jane. I allowed the party to proceed very quietly until I was left about ten yards behind; and then I ran with all my force on my sister Jane, — she fell with extended hands on the little page, he was thrown upon his father, and the grand chamberlain, to his dismay, was pushed against the emperor, who, although the shock was somewhat diminished by the time it reached him, had still some difficulty, from the steepness of the path, in preserving his footing. I was in ecstacies at the confusion I had created, and exulted in the revenge I had taken for the kiss; but I was soon obliged to change my note of triumph. Las Cases was thunderstruck at the insult offered to the emperor, and became perfectly furious at my uncontrollable laughter. He seized me by the shoulders, and pushed me violently on the rocky bank. It was now my turn to be enraged. I burst into tears of passion, and, turning to Napoleon, cried out, "Oh! sir, he has hurt me." "Never mind," replied the emperor, "ne pleurs pas — I will hold him while you punish him." And a good punishing he got; I boxed the little man's ears until he begged for mercy; but I would show him none; and at length Napoleon let him go, telling him to run, and that if he could not run faster than I, he deserved to be beaten again. He immediately started off as fast as he could, and I after him, Napoleon clapping his hands and laughing immoderately at our race round the lawn. Las Cases never liked me after this adventure, and used to call me a rude hoyden.

CHAPTER V

I never met with anyone who bore childish liberties so well as Napoleon. He seemed to enter into every sort of mirth or fun with the glee of a child, and though I have often tried his patience severely, I never knew him lose his temper or fall back upon his rank or age, to shield himself from the consequences of his own familiarity, or of his indulgence to me. I looked upon him, indeed, when with him, almost as a brother or companion of my own age, and all the cautions I received, and my own resolutions to treat him with more respect and formality, were put to flight the moment I came within the influence of his arch smile and laugh. If I approached him more gravely than usual, and with a more sedate step and subdued tone, he would, perhaps, begin by saying, "Eh bien, qu'as tu, Mademoiselle Betsee? Has le petit Las Cases proved inconstant? If he have, — bring him to me;" or some other playful speech, which either pleased or teased me, and made me at once forget all my previous determinations to behave prettily.

My brothers were at this time quite children, and Napoleon used to allow them to sit on his knee and amuse themselves by playing with his orders, etc. More than once he has desired me to cut them off to please them. One day Alexander took up a pack of cards, on which was the usual figure of the Great Mogul. The child held it up to Napoleon, saying, "See, Bony, this is you." He did not understand what my brother meant by calling him Bony. I explained that it was an abbreviation — the short for Bonaparte, but Las Cases interpreted the word literally, and said it meant a bony person. Napoleon laughed and said, "Je ne suis pas osseux," which he certainly never could have been, even in his thinnest days. His hand was the fattest and prettiest in the world; his knuckles dimpled like those of a baby, his fingers taper and beautifully formed, and his nails perfect. I have often admired its symmetry, and once told him it did not look large and strong enough to wield a sword. This led to the subject of swords, and one of the emperor's suite who was present, drew his sabre from the scabbard, and pointing to some stains on the blade, said, that it was the blood of Englishmen. The emperor desired him to sheath it, telling him it was bad taste to boast, particularly before ladies.

Napoleon then produced from a richly embossed case, the most magnificent sword I ever beheld. The sheath was composed of an entire piece of most splendidly marked tortoise-shell, thickly studded with golden bees. The handle, not unlike a fleur-de-lys in shape, was of exquisitely wrought gold. It was indeed the most costly and elegant weapon I had ever seen. I requested Napoleon to allow me to examine it more closely; and then a circumstance which had occurred in the morning, in which I had been much piqued at the emperor's conduct, flashed across me. The temptation was irresistible, and I determined to punish him for what he had done. I drew the blade out quickly from the scabbard, and began to flourish it over his head, making passes at him, the emperor retreating, until at last I fairly pinned him up in the corner; I kept telling him all the time that he had better say his prayers, for I was going to kill him. My exulting cries at last brought my sister to Napoleon's assistance. She scolded me violently, and said she would inform my father if I did not instantly desist; but I only laughed at her, and maintained my post, keeping the emperor at bay until my arm dropped from sheer exhaustion. I can fancy I see the figure of the grand chamberlain now, with his spare form and parchment visage, glowing with fear for the emperor's safety, and indignation at the insult I was offering him. He looked as if he could have annihilated me on the spot, but he had felt the weight of my hand before on his ears, and prudence dictated to him to let me alone.

When I resigned my sword, Napoleon took hold of my ear, which had been bored only the day before, and pinched it, giving me great pain. I called out, and he then took hold of my nose, which he pulled heartily, but quite in fun; his good humour never left him during the whole scene.

The following was the circumstance which had excited my ire in the morning. My father was very strict in enforcing our doing a French translation every day, and Napoleon would often condescend to look over them and correct their faults. One morning I felt more than usually averse to performing this task, and when Napoleon arrived at the cottage, and asked whether the translation was ready for him, I had not even begun it. When he saw this, he took up the paper and walked down the lawn with it to my father, who was preparing to mount his horse to ride to the valley, exclaiming as he approached, Balcombe, voilà le thême de Mademoiselle Betsee. Qu'elle a bien travaillé;" holding up at the same time the blank sheet of paper. My father comprehended imperfectly, but saw by the sheet of paper, and my name being mentioned by the laughing emperor, that he wished me to be scolded, and entering into the plot, he pretended to be very angry, and threatened if I did not finish my translation before he returned to dinner, I should be severely punished. He then rode off, and Napoleon left me, laughing at my sullen and mortified air, and it was the recollection of this which made me try and frighten him with the sword.

The emperor in the course of the evening desired a quantity of bijouterie to be brought down to amuse us; and amongst other things the miniatures of the young king of Rome.[8] He seemed gratified and delighted when we expressed our admiration of them. He possessed a great many portraits of young Napoleon. One of them represented him sleeping in his cradle, which was in the form of a helmet of Mars; the banner of France waved over his head, and his tiny right hand supported a small globe. I asked the meaning of these emblems, and Napoleon said he was to be a great warrior, and the globe in his hand signified that he was to rule the world. Another miniature, on a snuff-box, represented the little fellow on his knees before a crucifix, his hands clasped and his eyes raised to heaven. Underneath were these words: "Je prie le bon Dieu pour man pére, ma mére, et ma patrie." It was an exquisite thing. Another portrayed him with two lambs, on one of which he was riding, while the other he was decking out with ribbons. The emperor told us these lambs were presented to his son by the inhabitants of Paris. An unwarlike emblem, and perhaps intended as a delicate hint to the emperor to make him a more peaceable citizen than his papa. The paschal lamb, however, is, I believe, the badge on the colours of a distinguished English regiment, and perhaps may be intended to remind the soldier that gentleness and mercy are not inconsistent with the fiercer and more lion-like attributes of his profession. We next saw another drawing, in which the empress Maria Louisa and her son were represented, surrounded by a sort of halo of roses and clouds, which I did not admire quite so much as some of the others. Napoleon then said he was going to show us the portrait of the most beautiful woman in the world, and produced an exquisite miniature of his sister Pauline. Certainly I never saw anything so perfectly lovely. I could not keep my eyes from it, and told him how enchanted I was with it. He seemed pleased with my praises, and said it was a proof of taste, for she was perhaps one of the most lovely women that ever existed.

The emperor usually played cards every evening, and when we were tired of looking at the miniatures, etc., he said, "Now we will go to the cottage and play whist." We all walked down together. Our little whist table was soon formed, but the cards did not run smoothly, and Napoleon desired Las Cases to seat himself at a side table, and deal them until they dealt easily.

While the grand chamberlain was thus employed, Napoleon asked me what my *robe de bal* was to be. I must mention that on my father's refusal to allow me to go to the ball, which was to be given by Sir George Cockburn, I had implored the emperor's intercession for me. He most kindly asked my father to let me go, and his request, of course, was instantly acceded to. I now ran up stairs to bring my dress down to him. It was the first ball dress I had ever possessed, and I was not a little proud of it. He said it was very pretty; and the cards being now ready I placed it on the sofa, and sat down to play. Napoleon and my sister were partners, and Las Cases fell to my lot. We had always hitherto played for sugar-plums, but tonight Napoleon said, "Mademoiselle Betsee, I will bet you a Napoleon on the game." I had had a pagoda presented to me, which made up the sum of all my worldly riches, and I said I would bet him that against his Napoleon. The emperor agreed to this, and we commenced playing. He seemed determined to terminate this day of *espiéglerie* as he had begun it. Peeping under his cards as they were dealt to him, he endeavoured whenever he got an important one, to draw off my attention, and then slily held it up for my sister to see. I soon discovered this, and calling him to order, told him he was cheating, and that if he continued to do so, I would not play. At last he revoked intentionally, and at the end of the game tried to mix the cards together to prevent his being discovered, but I started up, and seizing hold of his hands, I pointed out to him and the others what he had done. He laughed until the tears ran out of his eyes, and declared he had played fair, but that I had cheated, and should pay him the pagoda; and when I persisted that he had revoked, he said I was *méchante* and a cheat; and catching up my ball dress from off the sofa, he ran out of the room with it, and up to the pavilion, leaving me in terror lest he should crush and spoil all my pretty roses. I instantly set off in chase of him, but he was too quick, and darting through the marquee, he reached the inner room and locked himself in. I then commenced a series of the most pathetic remonstrances and entreaties, both in English and French, to persuade him to restore me my frock, but in vain; he was inexorable, and I had the mortification of hearing him laugh at what I thought the most touching of my appeals. I was obliged to return without it. He afterwards sent down word he intended to keep it, and that I might make up my mind not to go to the ball. I lay awake half the night, and at last cried myself to sleep, hoping he would relent in the morning; but the next day wore away, and I saw no signs of my pretty frock. I sent several entreaties in the course of the day, but the answer was that the emperor slept, and could not be disturbed. He had given these orders to tease me. At last the hour arrived for our departure for the valley. The horses were brought round, and I saw the little black boys ready to start with our tin cases, without, alas! my beautiful dress being in them. I was in despair, and hesitated whether I should not go in my plain frock, rather than not go at all, when, to my great joy, I saw the emperor running down the lawn to the gate with my dress. "Here, Miss Betsee, I have brought your dress; I hope you are a good girl now, and that you will like the ball; and mind that you dance with Gourgaud." General Gourgaud was not very handsome, and I had some childish feud with him. I was all delight at getting back my dress, and still more pleased to find my roses were not spoiled. He said he had ordered them to be arranged and pulled out, in case any might have been crushed the night before. Napoleon walked by the side of our horses until he came to the end of the bridle-road which led to the Briars. He then stopped and remarked on the beauty of a house which was situated in the valley beneath us, asking to whom it belonged, and expressing his intention of going down to see it. Las Cases accompanied the emperor down the side of the mountain, and we went on to the ball. He mentioned the next day how charmed he had been with the plan, and that he had ridden home on a beautiful little Arab pony, belonging to the owner, Major Hodgson.[9]

CHAPTER VI

The only exception to the emperor's habits of regularity when with us was in his hour of rising. In the midst of our garden was a very large pond of transparent water, full of gold and silver fish; and near this was the grapery, formed of trellis-work, quite covered with vines of every description. At the end of the grapery was an arbour, round and over which a treillage of grapes clustered in the richest profusion. To this spot, which was so sheltered as to be cool in the most sultry weather, Napoleon was much attached. He would sometimes convey his papers there as early as four o'clock in the morning, and employ himself until breakfast time in writing; and, when tired of his pen, in dictating to Las Cases. No one was ever permitted to intrude upon him when there, and this little attention was ever after gratefully remembered.

From this prohibition, however, I was exempt, at the emperor's own desire. I was considered a privileged person. Even when he was in the act of dictating a sentence to Las Cases he would come and answer my call, "Come and unlock the garden door," and I was always admitted and welcomed with a smile. I did not abuse this indulgence, and seldom intruded on him when in his retreat I remember, however, one day, a very pretty young lady came from the valley to pass the morning with us: she was dying to see Napoleon, but the heat was very oppressive, and he had retired to his arbour to avoid it. I hesitated for some time between the fear of disturbing him and disappointing my friend; but at last Miss G. appeared so mortified at not seeing him, that I ran down to the garden and knocked at the door. For a long while I received no answer; but at length, by dint of thumping and calling to the emperor, I succeeded in waking him. He had fallen asleep in the arbour over his papers. He came up to the door, and asked me what I wanted. I said, "Let me in, and you shall know." He replied, "No; tell me first what it is, and then you shall come in." I was then obliged to say I wished to introduce a young lady to him. He declined seeing her, and desired me to say he was unwell. I told her she would be dreadfully disappointed, and that she was so pretty. "Not like the lady I was obliged to say agreeable things to yesterday?" he rejoined. I assured him she was quite a different person, being very young and handsome. At last I succeeded in getting the door opened. As soon as I found it unlocked, I ran up to the table where he had been writing and snatched up his papers. "Now," I said, " for your ill nature in keeping me so long at the door, I shall keep these, and then I shall find out all your secrets." He looked a little alarmed when he saw the papers in my hand, and told me to put them down instantly; but I refused, and set off round the garden, flourishing my trophies. At last he told me, if I did not give them up he would not be my friend, and I relinquished them. I then took hold of the emperor's hand, for fear he should escape, and led him to the house, where we found Miss C. I introduced her to Napoleon, and he delighted her excessively by his compliments on her beauty, etc. When she was going away, he walked down the lawn with her, and lifted her on to her horse. He told me, after she was gone, that she was a very pretty girl, but had the air of a *marchande de modes*.[10]

The golden fruit in this modern garden of Hesperides had for its dragon an old Malay slave, named Toby, who had been captured and brought to the island as a slave many years before, and had never since crossed its boundary. He was an original, and rather an interesting character. A perfect despot in his own domain, he never allowed his authority to be disputed; and the family stood almost as much in awe of him, as they did of the master of the Briars himself. Napoleon took a fancy to old Toby, and told papa he wished to purchase him, and give him his freedom; but for some political reason it was not permitted. The old man retained ever afterwards the most grateful sense of Napoleon's kindness, and was never more highly gratified than when employed in gathering the choicest fruit, and arranging the most beautiful bouquets, to be sent to Longwood, to "that good man, Bony," as he called the emperor. Napoleon made a point of inquiring, whenever I saw him, after the health of old Toby, and when he took his leave of him he presented him with twenty Napoleons.

The emperor was very accessible while at the Briars, and knowing how much it would delight us, he seemed to wish to return any little attentions we were able to offer him by courtesy and kindness to our friends. My father, one day, during his residence with us, invited a large party, and the emperor said he would join us in the evening. He performed his promise, and delighted every one with his urbanity and condescension. When any of our guests were presented to him, he usually inquired his profession, and then turned the conversation upon some topic connected with it. I have often heard wonder expressed at the extent of Napoleon's information, on matters of which he would hardly have been expected to know much. On this occasion, a very clever medical man, after a long conversation with the emperor on the subject of his profession, declared his astonishment to my father at the knowledge he possessed, and the clearness and brilliancy with which he reasoned on it, though his theories were sometimes rather heterodox. Napoleon told him he had no faith whatever in medicine, and that his own remedies were starvation and the warm bath. At the same time he professed a higher opinion of the medical, or rather surgical profession, than of any other. The practice of the law, he said, was too severe an ordeal for poor human nature, adding, that he who habituates himself to the distortion of truth, and to exultation at the success of injustice, will at last hardly know right from wrong; so it is, he remarked, with politics, a man must have a conventional conscience. Of the church, also, (*les ecclesiastiques*) he spoke harshly, saying that too much was expected from its members, and that they became hypocrites in consequence. As to soldiers, they were cut-throats and robbers, and not the less so because they were ready to send a bullet through your bead if you told them your opinion of them. But surgeons, he said, are neither too good nor too bad. Their mission is to benefit mankind, not to destroy, mystify, or inflame them against each other; and they have opportunities of studying human nature as well as of acquiring science. The emperor spoke in high terms of Lorrey,[11] who, he said, was a man of genius and of unimpeachable integrity.

On the emperor's first arrival in St. Helena, he was fond of taking exploring walks in the valley just below our cottage. In these short walks he was unattended by the officer on guard, and he had thus the pleasure of feeling himself free from observation. The officer first appointed to exercise surveillance over him when at Longwood was a Captain Poppleton,[12] of the 53rd regiment. It was his duty to attend him in his rides, and the orders given on these occasions were, "that he was not to lose sight of Napoleon." The latter was one day riding with Generals Bertrand, Montholon,[13] Gourgaud, and the rest of his suite, along one of the mountainous bridle-paths at St Helena, with the orderly officer in attendance. Suddenly the emperor turned short round to his left, and spurring his horse violently, urged him up the face of the precipice, making the large stones fly from under him down the mountain, and leaving the orderly officer aghast, gazing at him in terror for his safety, and doubt as to his intentions. Although equally well mounted, none of his Generals dared to follow him. Either Captain Poppleton could not depend on his horse, or his horse was unequal to the task of following

Napoleon, and giving it up at once, he rode instantly off to Sir George Cockburn, who happened at the time to be dining with my father at the Briars. He arrived breathless at our house, and, setting all ceremony aside, demanded to see Sir George, on business of the utmost importance. He was ushered at once into the dining-room. The Admiral was in the act of discussing his soup, and listened with an imperturbable countenance to the agitated detail of the occurrence, with Captain Poppleton's startling exclamation of "Oh! sir, I have lost the emperor." He very quietly advised him to return to Longwood, where he would most probably find General Buonaparte. This, as he prognosticated, was the case, and Napoleon often afterwards laughed at the consternation he had created. On Captain Poppleton's arriving at Longwood he found the emperor seated at dinner, and was unmercifully quizzed by him for the want of nerve he displayed in not daring to ride after him.

The emperor's vanity was flattered at having still the power to create fear, though a captive in such a prison as the impregnable island of St Helena. I have mentioned being struck with Napoleon's seat on horseback on first seeing him. He one day asked me whether I thought he rode well. I told him, and with the greatest truth, that I thought he looked better on horseback than anyone I had ever seen. He appeared pleased, and calling for his horse, he mounted and rode several times at speed round the lawn, making the animal wheel in a very narrow circle, and showing the most complete mastery over him.

One day, Archambault,[14] his groom, was breaking in a beautiful young Arab, which had been bought for the emperor's riding. The colt was plunging and rearing in the most frightful manner, and could not be induced to pass a white cloth which had been purposely spread on the lawn to break him from shying. I told Napoleon it was impossible that he could ever ride that horse, it was so vicious. He smiled, and beckoning to Archambault, desired him to dismount; and then, to my great terror, he himself got on the animal, and soon succeeded in making him not only pass the cloth, but put his feet upon it; and then rode him over and over it several times. Archambault, as it seemed to me, hardly knew whether to laugh or cry. He was delighted with his emperor's prowess, but mortified at his managing a horse so easily which he had been trying in vain to subdue. Napoleon mentioned that he had once ridden a favourite grey charger one hundred and twenty miles in one day. It was to see his mother, who was dangerously ill, and there were no other means of reaching her. The poor animal died in the course of the night. He said that his own power of standing fatigue was immense, and that he could almost live in the saddle. I am afraid to say how many hours he told me once he had remained on horseback, but I remember being much surprised at his powers of endurance. His great strength of constitution was probably more instrumental than one would imagine, at first view, in enabling him to reach the pinnacle of his ambition. The state of the mind is so dependent on the corporeal frame, that it is difficult to see how the kind of mental power which is necessary to success in war, or political turmoil, can exist without a corresponding strength of body, or at least of constitution. In how many critical periods of Napoleon's life would not the illness of a week have been fatal to his future schemes of empire! How might the sternness of purpose by which he subjugated his daring compeers of the revolution have been shaken, and his giant ambition thwarted, by a trivial sickness! The mind of even a Napoleon might have been prostrated, and his mighty will enfeebled, by a few days' fever. The successful leader of a revolution ought, especially, to be exempt from the evils to which flesh is heir; his very absence from the arena for a few days is enough to ruin him; depreciating reports are spread, the prestige vanishes, and he is pushed from his stool by some more vigorous and more fortunate competitor.

CHAPTER VII

The emperor possessed a splendid set of china, of the Sèvres manufacture, which had been executed at an enormous cost, and presented to him by the city of Paris. The service was now unpacking, and he sent for us to see them. They were painted by the first artists in Paris, and were most lovely. Each plate cost twenty-five Napoleons. The subjects all bore reference to his campaigns, or to some period of his early life. Many of them were battle pieces, in which the most striking incidents were portrayed with the utmost spirit and fidelity; others were landscapes, representing scenery connected with his victories and triumphs. One, I remember, made a great impression on me; it was a drawing of Napoleon on the bridge of Arcola — a slim youth, standing almost alone, with none near but the dead and dying who had fallen around him, was cheering on his more distant comrades to the assault. The emperor seemed pleased at my admiring it, and putting his hand to his side, exclaimed, laughing, "I was rather more slender then than I am now." The battle of Leipsic was one of the subjects depicted on the china. Napoleon's figure was happily done, and an admirable likeness; but one feels rather surprised at the selection of such a subject for a complimentary present. I believe the battle of Leipsic is considered to have been one of the most disastrous defeats on record, but probably the good citizens of Paris were not so well aware of this at the time the china was presented to him as they now are. His campaign in Egypt furnished subjects for some of the illustrations. The ibis was introduced in several of these Egyptian scenes, and happening to have heard that that bird was worshipped by the Egyptians, I asked him if it were not so. He smiled, and entered into a long narration of some of his adventures with the army in Egypt, advising me never to go there, as I should catch the ophthalmia and spoil my eyes. I had also heard that he had professed Mahometanism when there, and I had been prompted by some one to catechise him on the subject. I at once came out with the question in my Anglo-French, "Pourquoi avez vous tourné Turque." He did not at first understand me, and I was obliged to explain that "tourné Turque" meant changing his religion. He laughed and said, "What is that to you? Fighting is a soldier's religion; I never changed that. The other is the affair of women and priests; quant à moi, I always adopt the religion of the country I am in." At a later period some Italian ecclesiastics arrived at St Helena and were attached to Napoleon's suite.

Amongst the emperor's domestics at the Briars was a very droll character, his lamplighter, a sort of Leporello,[15] — a little fellow, most ingenious in making toys and other amusing mechanical contrivances. Napoleon would often send for the scaramouch[16] to amuse my brothers, who were infinitely delighted with his tricks and buffooneries. Sometimes he constructed balloons, which were inflated and sent up amidst the acclamations of the whole party. One day he contrived to harness four mice to a small carriage, but the poor little animals were so terrified that he could not get them to move, and after many ineffectual attempts, my brothers entreated the emperor to interfere. Napoleon told them to pinch the tails of the two leaders, and when they started the others would follow. This he did, and immediately the whole four scampered off, to our great amusement, Napoleon enjoying the fun as much as any of us, and delighted with the extravagant glee of my two brothers. I had often entreated the emperor to give a ball (before he left the Briars for Longwood) in the large room occupied by him, and which had been built by my father for that purpose. He had promised me faithfully he would, but when I pressed him urgently for the fulfilment of his word, he only laughed at me, telling me he wondered I could be so silly as to think such a thing possible. But I never ceased reproaching him for his breach of faith, and teased him so that at last, to escape my importunities, he said that as the ball was out of the question, he would consent, by way of *amende honorable*, to anything I chose to demand to console me for my disappointment.

"Dites moi — Que veux-tu que je fasse, Mademoiselle Betsee, pour te consoler?" I replied instantly, if you will play the game of blindman's buff, that you have so often promised me, I will forgive you the ball, and never ask for it again. Not knowing the French term (if there be any) for blindman's buff, I had explained before to the emperor the nature of the operation to be gone through. He laughed at my choice, and tried to persuade me to choose something else, but I was inexorable; and seeing his fate inevitable, he resigned himself to it with a good grace, proposing we should begin at once. My sister and myself, and the son of General Bertrand,[17] and some other of the emperor's suite formed the party. Napoleon said we should draw lots who should be blindfolded first, and he would distribute the tickets. Some slips of paper were prepared, on one of which was written the fatal word "la mort," and the rest were blanks. Whether accidentally, or by Napoleon's contrivance, I know not, but I was the first victim, and the emperor, taking a cambric handkerchief out of his pocket, tied it tightly over my eyes, asking me, if I could see. "I cannot see you," I replied; but a faint gleam of light did certainly escape through one corner, making my darkness a little less visible. Napoleon then taking his hat, waved it suddenly before my eyes, and the shadow and the wind it made, startling me, I drew back my head: "Ah, leetle monkee," he exclaimed in English, "you can see pretty well." He then proceeded to tie another handkerchief over the first, which completely excluded every ray of light. I was then placed in the middle of the room, and the game began. The emperor commenced by creeping stealthily up to me, and giving my nose a very sharp twinge; I knew it was he both from the act itself and from his footstep. I darted forward, and very nearly succeeded in catching him, but bounding actively away, he eluded my grasp. I then groped about, and, advancing again, he this time took hold of my ear and pulled it. I stretched out my hands instantly, and in the exultation of the moment screamed out, "I have got you — I have got you, now you shall he blindfolded!" but to my mortification it proved to be my sister, under cover of whom Napoleon had advanced, stretching his hand over her head. We then recommenced, the emperor saying that as I had named the wrong person, I must continue blindfolded. He teased and quizzed me about my mistake, and bantered me in every possible way, eluding at the same time, with the greatest dexterity, all my endeavours to catch him. At last when the fun was growing "fast and furious," and the uproar was at its height, it was announced that someone desired an audience of the emperor, and to my great annoyance, as I had set my heart on catching him and insisting on his being blindfolded, our game came to a conclusion.

CHAPTER VIII

The emperor having returned from seeing his visitor, and his dinner hour approaching, he invited us to dine with him. We told him we had already dined. "Then come and see me eat," he added, and when his dinner was announced by Cipriani,[18] we accompanied him to his marquee. When at table, he desired Navarre[19] to bring in some creams for me. I declined them, as I had dined, but I had, unfortunately, told him once before, that I was very fond of creams, and though I begged in vain to be excused, repeating a thousand times that I had dined and could eat no more, he pressed and insisted so strongly, that I was at last obliged to comply, and with some difficulty managed to eat half a cream. But although I was satisfied, Napoleon was not; and when I left off eating, he commenced feeding me like a baby, calling me his little bambina, and laughing violently at my woeful countenance. At last I could bear it no longer, and scampered out of the tent, the emperor calling after me, "Stop, Miss Betsee; do stay and eat another cream, you know you told me you liked them. The next day he sent in a quantity of *bon-bons* by Marchand,[20] with some creams, desiring his compliments to Mademoiselle Betsee, and intimating that the *creams* were for her.

The emperor possessed among his suite the most accomplished *confiseur* in the world. M. Piron daily supplied his table with the most elaborate, and really sometimes the most elegant designs in *pâtisserie* — spun sugar, and triumphal arches, and amber palaces glittering with prismatic tints, that looked as if they had been built for the queen of the fairies, after her majesty's own designs. Napoleon often sent us in some of the prettiest of these architectural delicacies, and I shall always continue to think the *bon-bons* from the atelier of Monsieur Piron more exquisite than anything I ever tasted. But I suppose I must grant, with a sigh, that early youth threw its *couleur de rose* tints over Piron's *bon-bons*, as well as over the more intellectual joys of that happy period. The emperor sometimes added sugared words, to make these sweet things sweeter.

On New Year's Day a deputation, consisting of the son of General Bertrand, Henri, and Tristan, Madame Montholon's little boy, arrived with a selection of *bon-bons* for us, and Napoleon observed that he had sent his Cupidons to the Graces. The *bon-bons* were placed in crystal baskets, covered with white satin napkins, on Sevres plates. The plates I kept till lately, when I presented them to a lady who had shown my mother and myself many very kind attentions; and they were some of the last presents I possessed of Napoleon's many little gifts to me, with the exception of a lock of his hair, which I still retain, and which might be mistaken for the hair of an infant, from its extreme softness and silkiness. Napoleon delighted in sending these little presents to ladies, and was generally courteous and attentive in his demeanour towards them. He always gave me the impression of being fond of ladies' society, and as Mr O'Meara remarks, when alluding to my sister and myself, dining one day with him, "his conversation was the perfection of *causerie*,[21] and very entertaining." He was, perhaps, rather too fond of using direct compliments, but this was very pardonable in one of his rank and country. He remarked once, that he had heard a great deal of the beauty and elegance of the Governor's daughter, and asked me who I thought the most beautiful woman in the island. I told him I thought Madame Bertrand superior, beyond all comparison to any one I had ever before seen. My father had been greatly struck with her majestic appearance on board the *Northumberland*, and I always thought everyone else sank into insignificance when she appeared; and yet her features were not regular, and she had no strict pretensions to beauty, but the expression of her face was very intellectual, and her bearing queen-like and dignified.

Napoleon asked me if I did not consider Madame Montholon pretty. I said, "No." He then desired Marchand to bring down a snuff box, on the lid of which was a miniature of Madame Montholon. It certainly was like her, and very beautiful. He told me it was what she had been, when young. He then recurred to Miss ———,[22] and said Gourgaud spoke in raptures of her, and had sketched her portrait from memory. He produced the drawing, and wished to know if I thought it a good likeness. I told him she was infinitely more lovely, and that it bore no trace of resemblance to her. I mentioned also that she was very clever and amiable. Napoleon said I was very enthusiastic in her favour, and had made him quite long to see her.

Mesdames Montholon and Bertrand, and the rest of his suite, often came to see him at the Briars, and remained there during the day. It was quite delightful to witness the deference and respect with which he was treated by them all. To them he was still "le grand empereur;" his every look was watched, and each wish anticipated, as if he had still been on the throne of Charlemagne.

On one of these occasions Madame Bertrand produced a miniature of the empress Josephine, which she showed to Napoleon. He gazed at it with the greatest emotion for a considerable time without speaking. At last, he exclaimed it was the most perfect likeness he had ever seen of her, and told Madame Bertrand he would keep it, which he did, until his death. He has often looked at my mother for a length of time very earnestly, and then apologized, saying that she reminded him so much of Josephine. Her memory appeared to be idolized by him, and he was never weary of excelling on her sweetness of disposition and the grace of her movements. He said she was the most truly feminine woman he had ever known. In speaking of the empress, he used to describe her as very subject to nervous affections when in the least degree indisposed or anxious; he often said she was the most amiable, elegant, charming, and affable woman in the world; and in the language of his native isle, asserted, "Era la dama la piu graziosa di Francia." She was the goddess of the toilet — all fashions originated with her, everything she appeared in, seemed elegant, and, moreover, she was so humane, and was the *best* of women. Still, with all the veneration he felt for her, he could not bear that it should be supposed she exercised the sway over his public actions attributed to her, and observed, "Although the Bourbons and English allow that I did some *good*, yet they generally qualify it by saying it was chiefly through the instrumentality of Josephine; when the fact was, that she never interfered with politics. In alluding to his divorce, he observed, nothing would have induced him to listen to such a measure but political motives; no other reason could have persuaded him to separate himself from a wife whom he so tenderly loved. But he thanked God she had died in time to prevent her witnessing his last misfortune. She was the greatest patroness of the fine arts that had been known in France for a series of years; she had frequently little disputes with Denon,[23] and even with himself, when she wanted to procure fine statues and pictures for her own gallery instead of the Museum. "But though I loved to attend to her whims, yet I always acted first to please the nation; and whenever I obtained a fine statue or valuable picture, I sent it there for the people's benefit. Josephine was grace personified; everything she did was marked with it. She never acted inelegantly during the whole time we lived together. Her toilet was perfection, and she resisted the inroads of time, to all appearance, by the exquisite taste of her *parure*."[24]

Napoleon afterwards spoke of the empress Marie Louise with great kindness and affection. He said she would have followed him to St Helena if she had been allowed, and that she was an amiable creature, and a very good wife. He possessed several portraits of her. They were not very attractive, and were seen to disadvantage when contrasted, as they generally were, with his own handsome and intellectual looking family.

The emperor retired early this evening. He had been in low spirits since receiving his visitor, and after the portraits of the empress Josephine and Maria Louisa had been produced, he appeared absorbed in mournful reflection, and was still more melancholy and dejected for the rest of the evening.

His visitor proved to be a Count Piontkowski,[25] a Polish officer, who had formerly held a commission in "la grande armée," and had landed in the morning, having with great difficulty obtained permission to follow his master into exile, "to share with him the vulture and the rock." He called at the Briars, and requesting an audience, information had been sent to the emperor of his arrival. A long interview took place between them, which apparently excited painful reminiscences in the mind of the exile. I asked him afterwards about his visitor; he seemed to have little personal recollection of him, but appeared gratified with his devotion, and observed, he had proved himself a faithful servant by following him into exile.

The emperor's English, of which he sometimes spoke a few words, was the oddest in the world. He had formed an exaggerated idea of the quantity of wine drunk by English gentlemen, and used always to ask me, after we had had a party, how many bottles of wine my father drank, and then laughing, and counting on his fingers, generally made the number five. One day, to annoy me, he said that my countrywomen drank gin and brandy; and then added, in English, "You laike veree mosh dreenk, Meess, sometimes brandee, geen." Though I could not help laughing at his way of saying this, I felt most indignant at the accusation, and assured him that the ladies of England had the utmost horror of drinking spirits, and that they were even fastidious in the refinement of their ideas and in their general habits. He seemed amused at my earnestness, and quoted the instance of a Mrs B——y, who had, in fact, paid him a visit once in a state of intoxication. It was singular, indeed, that one of the few English ladies he had ever been presented to should have been addicted to this habit. At last he confessed, laughing, that he had made the accusation only to tease me. When I was going away, he repeated, "You like dreenk, Meess Betsee; dreenk! dreenk!"

CHAPTER IX

As the time drew near, for Napoleon's removal from the Briars to Longwood, he would come into the drawing-room oftener, and stay longer. He would, he said, have preferred altogether remaining at the Briars; because he beguiled the hours with us better than he ever thought it possible he could have done on such a horrible rock as St Helena.

A day or two before his departure, General Bertrand came to the Briars and informed Napoleon that Longwood smelt so strongly of paint that it was unfit to go into. I shall never forget the fury of the emperor. He walked up and down the lawn, gesticulating in the wildest manner. His rage was so great that it almost choked him. He declared that the smell of paint was so obnoxious to him that he would never inhabit a house where it existed; and that if the grand marshal's report were true, he should send down to the admiral, and refuse to enter Longwood. He ordered Las Cases to set off early the next morning to examine the house and report if the information of General Bertrand was correct. At this time I went out to him on the lawn, and inquired the cause of his being in *such* a *rage*. The instant I joined him he changed his manner, and in a calm tone mentioned the reason of his annoyance. I was perfectly amazed at the power of control he evinced over his temper. In one moment, from the most awful state of fury, he subdued his irritability, and his manner became calm, gentle, and composed. Las Cases set off at daylight the next morning, and returned before twelve o'clock. He informed the emperor that the smell of paint was so slight as to be scarcely perceptible, and that a few hours would remove it altogether. The grand marshal was sharply reprimanded, as I afterwards learned, for making an exaggerated report. It was arranged that he should leave the Briars two days afterwards for Longwood, which was now quite ready for him.

On the appointed morning, which to me was a most melancholy one, Sir George Cockburn, accompanied by the emperor's suite, came to the Briars, to escort him to his new abode. I was crying bitterly, and he came up and said, "You must not cry, Mademoiselle Betsee; you must come and see me next week, and very often." I told him that depended on my father. He turned to him and said, "Balcombe, you must bring Missee Jane and Betsee to see me next week, eh? When will you ride up to Longwood?" My father promised he would, and kept his word. He asked where mamma was, and I said she desired her kind regards to the emperor, and regretted not being able to see him before his departure, as she was ill in bed. "I will go and see her;" and upstairs he darted before we had time to tell my mother of his approach. He seated himself on the bed, and expressed his regret at hearing she was unwell. He was warm in his acknowledgments of her attentions to him, and said, he would have preferred staying altogether at the Briars, if they would have permitted him. He then presented my mother with a gold snuffbox, and begged she would give it to my father as a mark of his friendship. He gave me a beautiful little bonbonniére, which I had often admired, and said you can give it as a *gage d'amour* to le petit Las Cases. I burst into tears and ran out of the room. I stationed myself at a window from which I could see his departure, but my heart was too full to look on him as he left us, and throwing myself on the bed, I cried bitterly for a long time.

When my father returned, we asked him how the emperor liked his new residence. He said that he appeared out of spirits, and, retiring to his dressing-room, had shut himself up for the remainder of the day.

From the circumstance that my father was the emperor's purveyor, we had a general order to visit Longwood, and we seldom allowed a week to pass without seeing him. On these occasions, we generally arrived in time to breakfast with him at one, and returned in the evening. He was more subject to depression of spirits than when at the Briars, but still gleams of his former playfulness shone out at times. On one occasion we found him firing at a mark with pistols. He put one into my hand, loaded, I believe, with powder, and, in great trepidation, I fired it off; he often called me afterwards "La petite tirailleure,"[26] and said he would form a corps of sharpshooters, of which I should be the captain. He then went into the house, and he took me into the billiard-room, a table having been just set up at Longwood. I remember thinking it too childish for men, and very like marbles on a larger scale. The emperor condescended to teach me how to play, but I made very little progress, and amused myself with trying to hit his imperial fingers with the ball instead of making cannons and hazards.

Napoleon's health and activity began to decline soon after his arrival at Longwood. In consequence of the unfortunate disputes with the governor, Sir Hudson Lowe,[27] his health became visibly impaired. He was unable; consequently, to enjoy that buoyancy of spirit Which had probably been the chief cause of his allowing me to be so often in his society, and of his distinguishing me with so much regard. But he never failed to treat me with the greatest tenderness and kindness.

Some months after his departure I was attacked with an alarming illness. Mr O'Meara attended me, and at one time despaired of my recovery. The emperor's kindness in making inquiries after me, and his other attentions, I can never forget. He ordered his confiseur, when I became convalescent, to supply me daily from his own table with every delicacy, to tempt my appetite and restore my strength.

CHAPTER X

With the assistance of my daughter's pencil, and some rough sketches I had by me, I have been enabled to give a view of the Briars, and the cottage occupied by Napoleon, whilst he stayed with us. He certainly appeared very contented during that time, and frequently expressed a strong desire that the government would permit him to remain there, by purchasing the estate; and on their refusing to do so, he sent General Montholon to negotiate with my father, that he himself might become the purchaser of the Briars: but circumstances (probably political) prevented the negotiation from being carried out. Napoleon used to watch with great interest the fatigue parties of the 53rd regiment, as they wound round the mountains, carrying on their shoulders the materials wherewith Longwood was to be rendered fit to receive him; and as the time of its completion drew nigh, he manifested his discontent by grumbling at the fifes and drums, to the sound of which the soldiers of the 53rd used to toil up those steep declivities, as their monotonous notes warned him of the speedy termination of his sojourn at our cottage.

Shortly after the emperor left the Briars, we proposed riding to Longwood, to see him, feeling exceedingly anxious to know how he was accommodated, and rather, it may be, hoping to hear him make a comparison in favour of the sweet place he had left for the sterile-looking domain in which his habitation was now placed; and I remember being in a state of ecstasy at the prospect of again beholding my old playmate — the loss of whose society I had so deeply regretted. We found him seated on the steps of his billiard-room, chatting to little Tristan Montholon.[28] The moment he perceived us, he started up and hastened towards us. Running to my mother, he saluted her on each cheek. After which fashion he welcomed my sister; but, as usual with me, he seized me by the ear, and pinching it, exclaimed, "Ah! Mademoiselle Betsee, êtes vous sage, eh, eh?" He then asked us what we thought of his palace, and bidding us follow him, said he would show us over his ménage. We were first conducted to his bedroom, which was small and cheerless.

Instead of paper hangings, its walls were covered with fluted nankeen;[29] and the only decorations I observed were the different portraits of his family, which on a former occasion he had shown to us. His bed was the little camp bedstead, with green silk hangings, on which he said he had slept when on the battlefields of Marengo and Austerlitz. The only thing approaching to magnificence in the furniture of this chamber, was a splendid silver wash-hand-stand basin and ewer. The first object on which his eyes would rest on awaking, was a small bust of his son, which stood on the mantel-piece, facing his bed, and above which hung a portrait of Marie Louise. We then passed on through an ante-room, to a small chamber, in which a bath had been put up for his use, and where he passed many hours of the day.

The apartments appropriated to him were the two I have just mentioned, with a dressing-room, dining-room, drawing-room, and billiard-room. The latter was built by Sir George Cockburn, and was the only well-proportioned room of which Longwood could boast.

After all these chambers were exhibited, and commented on by Napoleon, he proceeded with us to the kitchen, where he desired Piron the confectioner to send in some creams and bon-bons for Miss Betsee. Thence we went to the larder, where he directed our attention to a sheep that was hanging up, and said, laughingly, "Regardez — voilà un mouton pour mon diner, dont on a fait une lanterne." And sure enough, it was so — the French servants having placed a candle in its lean carcass, through which the light shone.

After we had gone all over the rooms, he conducted us to those of Madame Montholon, and introduced me to a little stranger — the countess's baby,[30] only then six weeks old, and which he began dandling so awkwardly, that we were in a state of terror lest he should let it fall. He occasionally diverted himself by pinching the little creature's nose and chin, until it cried. When we quizzed him for his *gaucherie*[31] in handling the child, he assured us he had often nursed the little King of Rome when he was much younger than the little Lili.

Before terminating our visit, Napoleon took us over the garden and grounds which surrounded his house. Nothing could exceed the dreariness of the view which presented itself from them; and a spectator unaccustomed to the savage and gigantic scenery of St Helena, could not fail to be impressed with its singularity. On the opposite side, the eye rested on a dismal and rugged-looking mountain, whose stupendous side was here and there diversified by patches of wild samphire, prickly pears, and aloes, serving to break but slightly the uniform sterility of the iron-coloured rocks, the whole range of which exhibited little more than huge apertures of caverns, and overhanging cliffs, which, in the early years of the colonization of the island, afforded shelter to herds of wild goats. I remember hearing Madame Bertrand tell my mother, that one of Napoleon's favourite pastimes was to watch the clouds as they rolled over the highest point of that gigantic mountain, and as the mists wreathed themselves into fantastic draperies around its summit, sometimes obscuring the valleys from sight, and occasionally stretching themselves out far to sea, his imagination would take wing, and indulge itself in shaping out the future from those vapoury nothings.

As a diversion to close the day, the emperor proposed a ride in his Irish jaunting car. Our horses were accordingly sent on to Hutsgate, the residence of Madame Bertrand; and accompanied by Napoleon, we set off at a hard gallop. I always was, and still am, the greatest coward in a carriage; and of all vehicles, that jaunting car seemed to me to be the one best calculated to inspire terror: it was driven by the fearless Archambault, with unbroken Cape horses, three abreast, round that most dangerous of roads called the Devil's Punchbowl. The party occupying the side nearest the declivity seemed almost hanging over the precipice, while the others were, apparently, crushed against the gigantic walls formed by the perpendicular rock. These were drives which seemed to inspire Bonaparte with mischievous pleasure. He added to my fright, by repeatedly assuring me the horses were running away, and that we should be all dashed to pieces. I shall never forget the joy I experienced on arriving in safety at Madame Bertrand's, and finding myself once more mounted on my quiet pony Tom.

After Napoleon had been on the island a few months, some newspapers arrived containing anecdotes of him, and all that occurred during his stay at the Briars: Amongst other *sottises*,[32] was a letter written by the Marquess de M———, in which he described all the romping games that had taken place between Napoleon and our family, such as blindman's buff, the sword scenes, and ending his communication by observing, that "Miss Betsee" was the wildest little girl he had ever met; and expressing his belief, that the young lady was *folle*.[33] This letter had been translated into the German and English journals. My father was much enraged at my name thus appearing, and wished to call the marquess to an account for his ill nature; but my mother's intercessions prevailed, and she obtained an ample apology from the marquess. On hearing of the affront that "Miss Betsee" had received from the *vieux imbecile*, as Napoleon generally denominated him, he requested Dr O'Meara would call at the Briars on his way to St James's Valley, with a message to me, which was to let me know how I might revenge myself. It so happened, that the marquess prided himself on the peculiar fashion of his wig, to which was attached a long cue. This embellishment to his head Napoleon desired me to burn off with caustic. I was always ready for mischief, and in this instance had a double inducement, on the emperor's promise to reward me, on the receipt of the pigtail, with the prettiest fan Mr Solomon's shop contained. Fortunately I was prevented indulging in this most hoydenish trick, by the remonstrances of my mother. The next time I saw the emperor, his first exclamation was, "Eh bien, Mademoiselle Betsee, a tu obéi mes ordres et gagné l'eventail?" In reply, I made a great merit of being too dutiful a daughter to disobey my mother, however much my inclinations prompted me to revenge the insult. He pinched my ear, in token of approval, and said, "Ah, Miss Betsee, tu commences à être sage." He then called Dr O'Meara, and asked him if he had procured the fan? The doctor replied, that there were none pretty enough. I believe I looked disappointed; on perceiving which, Napoleon, with his usual good nature, consoled me with the promise of something prettier — and he kept his word. In a few days I received a ring of brilliants, forming the letter N,[34] surmounted by a small eagle. The only revenge I took on the marquess, was by relating an anecdote of his greedy propensity, which diverted Napoleon very much. He was very fond of cauliflowers, which were rare vegetables in this island; dining with us one day at the Briars, his aide-de-camp, Captain Gor,[35] had omitted to point out to him that there were some at table; and it was only when about to be removed that the marquess espied the retreating dish. His rage was most amusing; and, with much gesticulation, he exclaimed, "Bête! pourquoi ne m'a tu pas dit qu'il y avait des choux-fleurs?"

During one of our riding excursions, we encountered Napoleon, who was returning from Sandy Bay, whither he had been to visit Mr D——, who resided there.[36] He expressed himself delighted with the place, and spoke in high terms of the urbanity of the venerable host of "Fairy Land." This gentleman had passed all his life at St Helena, and had at this time arrived at the advanced age of seventy, without ever having left the island. His appearance was most prepossessing; and to those who loved to revel in the ideal and imaginative, he might have been likened to a good genius presiding over the fairy valley in which he dwelt. A few years after the emperor's visit, Mr D was induced to come to England, and, thinking that he might never again return to his lovely and beloved valley, had a tree felled from his own "fairy land," from under the shade of which he had often viewed the enchanting scenery around, and had his coffin made from the wood. His arrival in England, together with his interesting character, being made known to the Prince Regent, afterwards George IV, his Royal

Highness desired that Mr D——— might be presented to him, and his Royal
Highness was so gratified with the interview, that he afterwards knighted
Mr D———, who subsequently returned to the island of which he was so
much enamoured.

I asked Napoleon if he had remarked, when at Sandy Bay, three singularly
formed rocks, shaped like sugar loaves, and called Lot's Wife and Daughters.
He replied, that he had. I then related to him an anecdote connected with the
largest of the three. More than half a century had elapsed since two slaves,
who preferred a freebooting life to one of labour and subjection, secreted
themselves in a cave half way up the declivity which terminates the spiral
rock called "Lot's Wife." From this stronghold their nocturnal sallies and
depredations were carried on with great success, and their retreat remaining
for a long while undiscovered, they became the terror of the island. They
were at length, however, tracked to their rocky hold, where they stood a
long siege, repelling all attacks by rolling stones on their assailants. It was
at last deemed necessary to send a party of soldiers, to fire on them if they
refused to surrender. But this measure was rendered unnecessary by the
superior activity of one of the besieging party, who managed to climb the
rock, reach the opposite side of the mountain, and clambering up still higher
to gain a situation above the cave, the mouth of which became thus exposed
to the same mode of attack which had effected its defence; so that, when
one of the unfortunate freebooters approached the edge of the precipice to
roll down stones, he was crushed to death, and his companions, who were
following him, severely wounded. Many of the islanders believe to this day,
that the ghost of the murdered slave is seen to make the circuit of the wild
spot wherein he carried on his nightly orgies — a superstition giving to an
"airy nothing a local habitation, and a name." In St Helena every cavern has
its spirit, and every rock its legend. Napoleon having listened to my legend
of the sugar-loaf mountain, said he should regard it with greater interest the
next time he rode in that direction.

CHAPTER XI

One of the many instances of Napoleon's great good nature, and his kindness in promoting my amusement, was on the occasion of the races at Deadwood, which had been instituted by the Honourable Henry John Rous,[37] the present member for Westminster, and which were at that time anticipated by the inhabitants of the island as a kind of jubilee. From having been, as was often the case, in arrears with my lessons, my father, by way of punishing me, declared that I should not go to the races; and fearing that he might be induced to break his determination, lent my pony Tom, to a friend of his for that day. My vexation was very great at not knowing where to get a horse, and I happened to mention my difficulty to Dr O'Meara, who told Napoleon; and my delight may be conceived when, a short time after all our party had left the Briars for Deadwood, I perceived the doctor winding down the mountain path which led to our house, followed by a slave leading a superb grey horse called "Mameluke," with a lady's side-saddle and housings of crimson velvet embroidered with gold. Dr O'Meara said that on telling the emperor of my distress, he desired the quietest horse in his stable to be immediately prepared for my use. This simply good-natured act of the emperor occasioned no small disturbance on the island, and sufficiently punished me for acting contrary to my father's wishes, by the pain it gave me to hear that he was considered to have committed a breach of discipline in permitting one of his family to ride a horse belonging to the Longwood establishment, and for which he was reprimanded by the governor.

We were told by Napoleon, the next day, that he had witnessed the races from the upper windows of General Bertrand's house, and expressed himself much amused by them. He said he supposed I was too much diverted by the gay scene to feel my usual timidity. The emperor frequently urged my father to correct me whilst young, and said I ought never to be encouraged in my foolish fears, or even permitted to indulge therein. He said the empress Josephine suffered the greatest terror in a carriage, and he mentioned several instances of her extreme fright, when he was obliged to reprimand her severely.

If I remember rightly, the Duchess D'Abrantes mentions in her memoirs of the emperor,[38] one of the anecdotes on this subject, which he recounted to us.

There was so very little to vary the monotony of Napoleon's life, that he took an interest in the most trifling attempts at gaiety in the island, and he generally consented to our entreaties to be present at some of the many entertainments which my father delighted in promoting. On one occasion, my father gave a fête to celebrate the anniversary of my birthday, at a pretty little place he possessed within the boundary of the emperor's rides, called "Ross Cottage," so named as being the abode, for a short time, of a highly esteemed friend, the flag captain of the *Northumberland*, whom Napoleon always designated as "un bravissimo uomo."[39] When the festivities were at their height, we descried the emperor riding along the hill's side towards the house, but on seeing such an assembly, he sent to say that he would content himself with looking at us from the heights above. I did not consider this was fulfilling his promise of coming to the party, and not liking to be so disappointed, I scampered off to where he had taken up his position, and begged he would be present at our festivity, telling him he must not refuse, since it was my birthday. But all my entreaties were unavailing; he said he could not make up his mind to descend the hill to be exposed to the gaze of the multitude, who wished to gratify their curiosity with the sight of him. I insisted, however, on his tasting a piece of birthday cake, which had been sent for that occasion by a friend from England, and who little knowing the strict surveillance exercised over all those in any way connected with the fallen chief and his adherents, had the cake ornamented with a large eagle; this, unluckily for us, was the subject of much animadversion.

I named it to Napoleon as an inducement for him to eat the cake, saying, "It is the least you can do for getting us into such disgrace." Having thus induced him to eat a thick slice, he pinched my ear; calling me a saucy simpleton, and galloped away humming, or rather attempting to sing, with his most unmusical voice, "Vive Henri Quatre."

One morning we went to call on Madame Bertrand, and found Napoleon seated by her bedside. We were about retreating, thinking we had been shown into a wrong room, when he called out in his imperfect English, desiring us to enter, and asked what we were afraid of, saying, "I am visiting my dear loaf, my mistress." My mother observed that the latter term had a strange signification, and that it was never used in our language to express friendship. He laughed heartily at the awkward error he had made, and promised not to forget the interpretation of the word for the future, repeating that he only meant to express that Madame Bertrand was his dear friend.

It was by Napoleon's especial desire that we ventured now and then to correct his English, and being very anxious to improve himself, he never let an opportunity pass when in our society without trying to converse in English, though, from his exceedingly bad pronunciation and literal translations, it required the most exclusive attention to understand him. For my part, I seldom had patience to render him much assistance, my sister being generally obliged to finish what I had begun, for in the middle of his lesson I would walk away attracted by some more frivolous pursuit; on returning I was always saluted with a tap on the cheek or a pinch of the ear, with the exclamation of "Ah! Mademoiselle Betsee, petite étourdie que vous êtes, vous ne devenez jamais sage." Bonaparte on one occasion asked us if we had seen little Arthur, who was about a month old, and he repeated Madame Bertrand's speech on introducing the child to him: "Allow me to present to your majesty a subject who has dared to enter the gates of Longwood without a pass from Sir Hudson Lowe."

He sat a long time chatting, and quizzing me about the short waist and petticoats of my frock. He took great pleasure in teasing me about my trousers, and calling me a little boy, which he always made a point of doing whenever he espied the trousers. He thought the fashion of wearing short waists very frightful, and said if he were governor, he should issue an order that the ladies were not to appear dressed in that style. Before leaving Madame Bertrand's cottage, he joined the children in a game of "puss in the corner,"[40] to which I acted as *maîtresse de ballet*.

Napoleon used to evince great curiosity about the subject of our conversations, when we called on Lady Lowe at Plantation House, and asked whether they discussed our visits to Longwood. I told him that the same sort of interrogation went on there, and that I was sure to be sharply (though good-naturedly) cross-questioned about what we did and what we heard, when in his presence.

One evening, whilst on a visit to Madame Bertrand, we strolled up to see Dr O'Meara, who happened to be engaged with the emperor; Cipriani, however, sent in to say that some ladies were waiting to see him, and on Napoleon hearing our names, he requested us to come in. We found him in the billiard-room, employed looking over some very large maps, and moving about a number of pins, some with red heads, others with black. I asked him what he was doing. He replied that he was fighting over again some of his battles, and that the red-headed pins were meant to represent the English, and the black to indicate the French. One of his chief amusements was going through the evolutions of a lost battle, to see if it were possible by any better manoeuvring to have won it.

CHAPTER XII

A ball occasionally given by the officers of the 66th regiment, afforded some variety to the dreariness of Madame Bertrand's changed existence. One of these took place whilst we were on a visit to her, and it was arranged that we should go together in Napoleon's carriage, after dining with the emperor, as he said he wished to criticise our dresses, and then proceed from his door to the ball.

Madame Montholon very good naturedly sent her maid Josephine to arrange my hair.[41] She combed and strained it off my face, making me look like a Chinese. It was the first time I had seen such a coiffure, and I thought I had never beheld anything so hideous in my life, and would gladly have pulled it all down, but there was no time, and I was obliged to make my appearance before Napoleon, whose laugh I dreaded, with my eyes literally starting from my head, in consequence of the uneasy manner in which my hair had been arranged. However, to my great comfort, he did not quiz it, but said it was the only time he had ever seen it wear the appearance of anything like neatness. But my little leno[42] frock did not pass muster so well: he declared it was frightful, from its extreme shortness, and desired me to have it lengthened. In vain I pleaded the impossibility of any alteration; he kept twitching it about, until I was obliged to fly to Josephine, and have the desired change made by letting down some of the tucks, thereby spoiling the effect of my pretty dress; but I knew it was useless resisting, when once the fiat had gone forth.

After dinner the carriage was announced, and we all obeyed the emperor's signal of rising from table, his manner of performing that ceremony being brusque and startling. He would push his chair suddenly away, and rise as if he had received an electric shock. I recollect his remarking upon the want of gallantry displayed by Englishmen, in sitting so long after dinner. He said, "If Balcombe had been here, he would want to drink one, two, three, ah! cinq bouteilles, eh? Balcombe go to the Briars to get droonk?" It was one of his early attempts at expressing himself in English. I think I can see him now, holding up one of his exquisitely taper fingers, and counting how many bottles my father usually drank before he joined the ladies. "If I were you, Mrs Balcombe," he said, addressing my mother, "I should be very angry at being turned out to wait for two or three hours, whilst your husband and his friends were making themselves drunk. How different are Frenchmen, who think society cannot be agreeable without the presence of ladies!"

After drinking some of La Page's[43] delectable coffee, and being helped to the sugar by Napoleon's fingers, instead of silver tongs, we proceeded to the carriage, which was in waiting. Madame Bertrand led the way, carrying her baby, little Arthur, followed by my mother, my sister and myself, and General Gourgaud. On being seated, the signal was given, the whip applied to the spirited Cape steeds, and away they tore, first on one side of the *track* (for road there was none) and then on the other, Madame Bertrand screaming with all her power for Auchambault to stop; but it was not until a check was put to the velocity of the carriage, by its coming in contact with a large gum-wood tree, that we had any chance of being heard. At length the door was opened, and out we scrambled, up to our knees in mud, the night being wet and foggy. We had nearly a mile to walk through this filthy road to Deadwood, and the poor Countess all the while carrying her infant, who would not be pacified with any other nurse. I never shall forget the figure we cut on arriving at Mr Baird's quarters, where we were provided with dry clothes; nor the ludicrous appearance of Madame Bertrand, habited in one of Mrs Baird's dresses, which was half a yard too short, and much too small in every way. Mrs Baird being remarkably *petite*, whilst the Countess was *renommée* for her tall and graceful stature. But in spite of our adventure and *contretemps*, we had a very merry ball, and the party did not separate until long after the booming guns from the forts around announced the break of day. We cared little for our walk home through the mist and rain, as we knew that on arriving at the Grand Marshal's cottage we should be refreshed by a good breakfast and comfortable beds. Napoleon complimented me on my dancing and appearance at the ball, which he had heard were much admired, and also told me that I was considered very like Baroness Sturmer,[44] and might be mistaken for her young sister. I was flattered at the resemblance, as I thought her the prettiest woman I had ever seen.

I had been to a breakfast given to Lord Amherst,[45] (the British ambassador to the Chinese empire,) on board the *Newcastle*, where this fête was held, the entertainers being Sir Pulteney and Lady Malcolm.[46] On next visiting Longwood, I was surprised and vexed to find that the emperor had heard an account of the party from other lips than mine, as I was anxious to forestall the narration of the exploits of a certain hoydenish young lady, namely, myself; but he had received a faithful detail of them from Dr O'Meara. He pretended to scold and take me to task for being such a *petite folle*, and said he hoped the account were not true; he then began recapitulating the offences of which I had been guilty, to my father, stating that I had teased and locked up pretty little Miss P., while the ladies were being whipped[47] over the side of the frigate to return to the shore, and it was not until we had nearly reached the fort that the fair lady's absence was perceived, when, it being inconvenient to return the barge, it was proposed to Captain G., one of the party, and a great admirer of the young lady, that he should proceed to the frigate and rescue the terrified girl. Napoleon said, "Miss Betsee must be punished for being so naughty. N'est ce pas, Balcombe?" turning to my father, whom he requested to set me a task, to be repeated to him on my next visit; such a request my father was of course delighted to put into execution, being only too happy to have an excuse to make me study. On hearing what was in store for me, I assured him I had been sufficiently punished already for my cruelty to Miss P., having been really frightened out of my little wits by the roaring of the cannon from every fort which overhung the bay, and from all the men-of-war stationed in the harbour, to salute Lord Amherst on his landing. I also mentioned the scolding I had received from Lady Lowe, who kept desiring me to use my reason, and "not to be so childish."

Napoleon did not lose the opportunity of attacking Lady Lowe, though at my expense, and said he wondered at her ladyship's want of perception in giving me credit for what I never possessed. I amused Bonaparte that day by my ecstasies in describing the impression the courtier-like manner and charming address of Lord Amherst had made on me. He seemed pleased at my entertaining the same idea as himself, and said, "The ambassador must have been fascinating to have impressed your youthful fancy."

From the strict surveillance exercised over the emperor, the inconveniences suffered by his suite were, on many occasions, extremely annoying, and I quote the following as an instance:— my sister and I were constantly in the habit of staying with Madame Bertrand, who kindly volunteered, during my long visits to her, to superintend my studies. Upon one occasion, at her request, I attempted to sing a little French romance, composed by Hortense Beauharnois, daughter to the empress Josephine, entitled, "Le depart des Styriens." This song had been sent to her the preceding evening by Napoleon, who was anxious to hear it, and intimated that he should come for that purpose. He came according to promise, but was not only disappointed but angry at the discordant sounds that issued from the piano, which, from damp and disuse, had acquired tones very like those of a broken down hurdy-gurdy. The only person on the island capable of remedying the defects of the instrument, was Mr Guinness,[48] band-master on board the *General Kid*, then lying in the St James's harbour. Mr Guinness, who, at the request of the countess was summoned by my father for the purpose, was on the point of leaving the side of the ship, when an order from the governor desired him to stay where he was.

Napoleon expressed a wish to see a boa constrictor brought by Captain Murray Maxwell to the island. I had described its gorging a goat, and the extraordinary appearance it presented after such a meal. The horns of the unfortunate animal, which had been put alive into the cage, seemed as if they must protrude through the snake's skin. The emperor observed, that he thought, from what he had heard, that the Marquess de M——, from the quantity of food he consumed, must resemble a boa constrictor. I understood that it was not thought advisable to comply with the emperor's wish to have the monster conveyed to Longwood.

Early one morning, whilst I was wandering about the gardens and plantations at Longwood, I encountered the emperor, who stopped, told me to come with him, and he would show me some pretty toys. Such an invitation was not to be resisted, and I accordingly accompanied him to his billiard-room, where he displayed a most gorgeously carved set of chess-men, which had been presented to him by Mr Elphinstone.[49] He might well call them toys, every one being in itself a gem. The castles, surmounting superbly chased elephants, were filled with warriors in the act of discharging arrows from their bended bows; the knights were cased in armour, with their visors up, and mounted on beautifully caparisoned horses; mitred bishops appeared in their flowing robes; and every pawn was varied in character and splendour of costume, each figure furnishing a specimen of the dress of some different nation. Such workmanship had never before left China: art and taste had been exerted to the utmost to devise such rare specimens of skill and elegance. The emperor was as much pleased with his present as I should have been with a new plaything. He told me he had just finished a game of chess with Lady Malcolm,[50] with these most beautiful things, and that she had beaten him; he thought, solely from his attention having been occupied in admiring the men; instead of considering the game. The work-boxes and card-counters were lovely: the latter representing all the varied trades of China, minutely executed in carving. These gifts were presented to Napoleon, as a token of gratitude, by Mr. Elphinstone, from the circumstance of the emperor having humanely attended to his brother, when severely wounded on the field of Waterloo — on which occasion Napoleon sent for his refreshment a goblet of wine from his own canteen, on hearing he was faint from the loss of blood.[51] Napoleon observed, that he thought the chess-men too pretty for St Helena, and that therefore he should transmit them to the King of Rome. Another present which attracted my attention, was a superb ivory tea chest, which, when open, presented a perfect model of the city of Canton, most ingeniously manufactured of stained ivory; underneath this tray were packets of the finest tea, done up in fantastic shapes. Napoleon told me, that when he was Emperor of France he did not permit any tea to be drunk in his dominions except that grown in Switzerland, which so nearly resembled the Chinese plant that the difference was not perceptible. He also cultivated the growth of beetroot, for the purpose of making sugar, instead of depending upon foreign produce.

Seeing the ex-emperor one day less amiable than usual, and his face very much swollen and inflamed, I inquired the cause, when he told me that Mr O'Meara had just performed the operation of drawing a tooth, which caused him some pain. I exclaimed, "What! — you complain of the pain so trifling an operation can give? You, who have passed through battles innumerable, amid storms of bullets whizzing around you, and by some of which you must occasionally have been hit! I am ashamed of you. But, nevertheless, give me the tooth, and I will get it set by Mr Solomons[52] as an ear-ring, and wear it for your sake." The idea made him laugh heartily, in spite of his suffering, and caused him to remark, that he thought I should *never* cut my wisdom teeth; — he was always in extra good humour with himself whenever he was guilty of anything approaching to the nature of a witticism.

Napoleon had a peculiar horror of ugly women, and knowing this weakness, I one day begged he would allow me to introduce to him a Mrs S., the wife of a gentleman holding a high official appointment in India. I must confess feeling rather nervous at the time, knowing her to be one of the very plainest persons ever seen. She had, nevertheless, all the airs and graces of a beauty, and believed herself to be as lovely as Chinerey had portrayed her on ivory. She thought she might make an impression on the great man, and for that purpose loaded herself with all the finery an Indian wardrobe could afford. She dressed in crimson velvet bordered with pearls, and her black hair she braided and adorned with pearls, and butterflies composed of diamonds, rubies, and emeralds. When introduced to Napoleon, and after he had put the usual questions to her, as to whether she were married, how many children she had, and so on; he scrutinised her over and over again, trying, but in vain, to discover some point whereon to compliment her; at last he perceived that she had an immense quantity of coarse, fuzzy, black hair, which he remarked, by saying to her, "Madame, you have most luxuriant hair." The lady was so much pleased with this speech of the emperor's, that on her arrival in England she published in the newspapers an account of her interview with him, and said "Napoleon had lost his heart to her beauty." I really did incur the emperor's displeasure for a few days by the trick I had played him, having led him to suppose he was about to see a perfect Venus; and he prohibited me from ever introducing any more ladies to him.

CHAPTER XIII

Napoleon was very anxious about hearing any gossip relative to picnics, balls, or parties, that took place at St Helena, and always made me recount to him what we did, who we met, and who were my partners. He once asked me who danced the best at the governor's balls; and on my replying Mrs Wilks, the governor's lady, he was anxious to know what sort of dances were the fashion there. I described our quadrilles and country dances, which had been introduced by a Mr C——, the greatest beau that ever came to St Helena. This youth was such an exquisite, that he would sit with his feet elevated considerably above his head for an hour before dressing for dinner, that he might squeeze them the more readily into tight shoes; he wore his epaulette nearly down to his elbow; and his sword belt was embroidered with golden oak leaves. The same kind of embroidery confined his silk stocking round each knee, where it resembled the order of the garter. His disgust was very great at finding the St Helena ladies understand nothing but *kitchen* dances, and reels; and he immediately began to drill, and, after much toil, succeeded in instructing them in the mysteries of the quadrille figures. Once, whilst he was figuring away in the capacity of dancing master, my mother very unceremoniously put her foot on his heel, because he stood bending before her, and nearly extinguishing her eye with the swallow tails of his uniform coat. The perplexity this occasioned him was considerable, from the difficulty he had in thrusting his foot again into its tiny case.

Napoleon was so amused with our description of young C——, that he begged us to bring him to Longwood, if he could get a pass; one was accordingly procured; and as the emperor's eye rested on him, putting on a most comical look, he told him that he had heard from Miss Betsee that he was a great *dandy*, — which was anything but pleasing intelligence to the young hero, who began to think he was indebted for the honour of his interview with the great man to the circumstance of his being considered a sort of tom-fool. Napoleon, suiting his conversation (which, as I have before said, he always did) to his company, began admiring the cut of his coat, and said, "You are more fortunate than myself, for I am obliged to wear my coat turned;" this had really been the case, as no cloth could be procured on the island of the shade of green worn by Napoleon and his suite. Young C's interview with the great man, however, ended very satisfactorily to both; for, although a little too conceited, he was very gentlemanly, spoke French fluently, and left a pleasing impression on the exile of Longwood.

One morning, my father told me he was going to Longwood, and had been requested by the emperor to bring myself and sister to see him, as he had something curious to show us. We were only too happy to obey his wishes; and the next day saw us at Longwood. He reproached us for having so long neglected to pay him a visit, and wished to know why we had absented ourselves so much from him: on my telling him, I had but just recovered from a slight attack of *coup de soleil*, he was quite cheering in his sympathy. I told him it had been occasioned by my walking with Captain Mackey and my sister to call on Mrs Wilks, and that our way led over the high mountain at the back of the Briars, called Peak Hill. It was certainly a tremendous undertaking for one so young to attempt. The mountain is not accessible to four-footed animals, and is 2000 feet in height, and nearly perpendicular. Imagine, therefore, our toiling to its summit, and descending to the deep valley beneath, crossing Francis Plain, and ascending two mountain ridges, before terminating our expedition! We arrived at Plantation House worn and weary; but when once there, the kindness of the lady governess, and the care and attention of her amiable and lovely daughter, soon made us forget our fatigues; and at noon of that same day we started for Sir William D——'s[53] lovely valley of "Fairy Land." I described all our adventure, and the kindness we had received from Mrs Wilks at Plantation House, and from Miss D—— at Fairy Land. A few days after Napoleon invited the former lady, with her husband and daughter, to Longwood, but from political reasons the honour of the interview was declined. The wonderful exhibition we were invited to see, was the process of turning water into ice by one of Leslie's machines, sent out to Napoleon for that purpose;[54] he explained the process to us, and tried to enlighten me as to the principle upon which air-pumps were formed; he advised me, moreover, to get a book upon elementary chemistry, for my amusement and improvement; and finished, as usual, by turning to my father, recommending him to enforce a lesson every day, and directing the good O'Meara, as he called his doctor, to be my examiner. After making a cup of ice, he insisted upon my putting a large piece into my mouth, and laughed to see the contortions it induced from the excessive cold. It was the first ice that had ever been seen at St Helena; and a young island lady, Miss

De F——,[55] who was with us, would not believe that the solid mass in her hand was really frozen water, until it melted and streamed down her fingers. I recollect ending the morning's diversions by cutting from Napoleon's coat an embroidered bugle, and running away with it as a trophy. I now regret that I did not keep it; but, like most other relics and valuable mementos, I gave it away — it was attached to the coat he wore at Waterloo.

The emperor asked me one day, whether I was acquainted with Captain Wallis,[56] who commanded the *Podargus*; and on my replying in the affirmative, he said, somewhat abruptly, "What does he think of me?" It so happened, that, in the case of this officer, the prejudice against Napoleon (and indeed against everything French, at that time common to all Englishmen) was sharpened, upon the whetstone of painful experience, into the acuteness of rancour and bitter hatred; perhaps the word prejudice is hardly a fit term to apply to that particular mania which then existed, — a feeling which, first instilled into our infant minds by our nurses, "grew with our growth, and strengthened with our strength," until it fully ripened into that settled jealousy, which was but too apparent in all the transactions which took place between the individual inhabitants of the hostile countries. It was, therefore, not without the assistance of all my small stock of girlish assurance that I ventured to answer, "Oh! he has the most abominable opinion of you in the world; he says that you shut him up for ten years in the Temple, and there is no end to the barbarities that he lays to your charge. He declared to us, that, on one occasion, they removed him from one cell to another, which had been just vacated by the corpse of a man who had shot himself through the head, and that he met the body on the way. Moreover, his gaolers had not the decency to wash away the dead man's brains, which had been scattered on the wall, but left them there for the special annoyance of the living Occupant. Besides that, he accuses you of nearly starving him: to such an extent did he suffer from want of food, that he and Captain Shaw, a follow-sufferer, once tore a live duck to pieces, and devoured it like cannibals."

The emperor observed, that it was not to be wondered at that Captain Wallis was so inveterate against him, as he was the lieutenant who, together with Wright, had been convicted of landing spies and brigands in his territories, for which they were afterwards reported to have been murdered by his (the emperor's) orders. The conspiracy of Georges, Moreau and Pichegru, in which Captains Wright and Wallis were supposed to have been mixed up, has been so often described, and so ably discussed, that there are few who have taken an interest in the history of Napoleon, but must be well acquainted with all the circumstances connected with it. I remember being greatly interested with Wallis's narrative of his escape from prison, as it was told to us by him. Although years have passed since I heard it, still it is as freshly graven on my memory as when first my wondering ears listened to the exciting history. After ten long years of dreary captivity, urged by that powerful stimulus which hope builds upon despair, with the assistance of a rusty knife which he had contrived to conceal from his gaoler, he succeeded in moving one of the bars from his prison windows. The first great obstacle being removed, he found he had to overcome another, not less formidable. A hundred feet beneath the aperture which his patience and skill had succeeded in making large enough for his egress, flowed the still, dark waters of the Seine. As a drowning man catches at a straw, so did he seize upon whatever was likely to break his fall; and with a rope of no greater length and thickness than he was able to make out of his linen, he lowered himself as far as it would reach. The leap was fearful, but the very walls he touched gave him a convulsive shudder, when they brought to his mind the horrors of captivity and its concomitant evils, of which starvation was not the least. The splash of his fall into the water was loud enough to rouse the sentinels; he was senseless from its stunning effects for some seconds, and when he came to himself, struck out for the opposite bank. The bullets whizzed round him in all directions, but the darkness of the night was sufficient protection, and he gained the friendly shore in safety. By the aid of an accomplice, he obtained a pedlar's dress, in which, after numberless hair-breadth escapes, he reached the coast, and was taken on board an English frigate. He was afterwards appointed to the *Podargus*, and sent to cruise off St Helena, he being, naturally enough, supposed to be the best guard to set over one, whom he hated as deeply as he did Napoleon.

We always made a point of riding to Longwood every New Year's day, to wish the emperor a happy new year, and we dined with him or Madame Bertrand, though more frequently with the former. I recollect one New Year's day I had been anticipating a present from the emperor all the morning, and as the day wore on, my hopes began to wax faint, and I was beginning to make up my mind to have nothing new and pretty to feast my eyes upon, when Napoleon himself waddled into Madame Bertrand's room, where my sister and I were seated, and perhaps rather enviously viewing some elegant souvenirs of which the emperor had made the countess a present that morning. In his hand were two beautiful Sévres cups, exquisitely painted, one representing himself in Egypt, in the dress of a Mussulman; upon the other was delineated an Egyptian woman drawing water. "Here, Mesdemoiselles Betsee and Jane, are two cups for you; accept them as a mark of the friendship I entertain for you both, and for your kindness to Madame Bertrand." Oh! how delighted I was with my beautiful gift; I would not trust it out of my hand, but rode with it wrapped in cotton all the way home, for fear of its being injured. It always brought a smile to Napoleon's countenance, whenever he gave pleasure to the young around him.

One day, before the emperor had left my father's, we were walking with him down the Pomegranate Walk which led to the garden, when suddenly the voices of strangers were heard, and he began running away as fast as he could towards the garden gate, but found it locked from within. The strangers' steps approached nearer and nearer, and Napoleon had nothing left for it, but to jump over the garden fence, which, unfortunately, was defended on the top by the prickly pear, a plant covered with thorns. When he found himself on the top, there he stuck, the thorny bush preventing his extricating himself. At length, after a considerable struggle, torn clothes, and with his legs much scratched, the discomfited emperor descended on the garden side of the hedge, before the advancing company surprised him. The wounds he received that day were of no trifling nature, and it required a little of Dr O'Meara's skill to extract the thorns which the prickly pears had deposited in his imperial person.

Napoleon always evinced great kindness and interest for those who were ill, and his sympathy was much excited in the case of Captain Meynell[57] who had a very severe and dangerous illness during the time he was stationed at St Helena. I recollect perfectly whilst he was ill, under my father's roof, that Napoleon's *maître d'hôtel*, Cipriani, came every day to inquire after him. When we saw the emperor, a few days after Captain Meynell left us, we told him that he had been moved to Plantation House, where he would have more room and better attention than at our cottage, and that he was so ill as to be obliged to be removed in his cot; he had a relapse, and his life was despaired of. The emperor begged, when next we saw Lady Lowe, we would send him word how the brave Captain was.

CHAPTER XIV

Napoleon was fond of sailors, and liked entering into conversation with the young midshipmen who conducted the fatigue parties at Longwood. On one occasion a remarkably handsome and high-born young reefer attracted his notice, from the activity he displayed in setting his men to work in erecting a commodious marquee out of a studding-sail. He inquired his name, and when he heard it was the Honourable G. C.,[58] he remarked that he was one of the very few instances in which he had observed high birth combined with so much amiability and intelligence. We told the emperor we had the pleasure of being acquainted with the young middy he so much admired, and that he was the most popular of any of his young companions in the wardroom. I related to the emperor our first introduction to him, which was on our return from the admiral's ball, when we saw him elevated in a cart, surrounded by his brother middies, shouting at the top of his voice, "Lord W.'s carriage stops the way;" and true enough the way was stopped, as the cart had been dragged by some of these wild boys within the arch of the castle, through which we had all to pass on our road homeward. The next time we heard of him our sympathies were excited by hearing he had narrowly escaped being drowned, and afterwards being very nearly shot, when rowing guard one night. The surf was dangerously high, compelling his boat to keep off shore, and when hailed by the sentry, the roaring of the sea against the iron-girt rocks, prevented the countersign from being heard; the guard then fired in amongst the crew, but our gallant young friend most providentially escaped with his life.

We concluded our history of the middy by telling Napoleon, that his talent was equally distinguished in performing his duties either on sea or laud, and that Sir Pulteney Malcolm had made a farmer of him, entrusting to his management the superintendence and cultivation of one of the government farms. The admiral declared he had never before seen such vegetables produced on the sterile rock of St Helena. Napoleon's concluding remark was, that "Whatever British sailors took in hand, they never left undone."

When we were visiting Madame Bertrand's, we always passed our Sundays as if at home, reading the lessons for the day and observing the prayers, etc. One Sunday morning, Napoleon came bustling in, and seeing me very earnestly employed reading aloud to my sister, asked what I was so intently engaged upon, and why I looked so much graver than usual. I told him I was learning to repeat the collect for the day, and that if I failed in saying it, my father would be very angry. I remarked, "I suppose *you* never learnt a collect or any thing religious, for I am told you disbelieve the existence of a God." He seemed displeased at my observation, and answered, "You have been told an untruth; when you are wiser you will understand that no one could doubt the existence of a God." My mother asked him if he was a predestinarian, as reported. He admitted the truth of the accusation, saying, "I believe that whatever a man's destiny calls upon him to do, that he must fulfil."

Dr O'Meara often amused us by recounting conversations he had with the emperor respecting priestcraft: one anecdote is impressed on my recollection from the amusement it afforded. A poor erring monk having paid the debt of nature, a funeral oration was delivered by a brother priest, to a large assembled congregation. The holy father proceeded to inform the multitude that the soul of the departed had had to appear before the judgment-seat, there to render an account of all its past actions; that being done, the evil and the good were then separated and thrown into opposite scales, in order to see which preponderated. The good deeds were so few, that the scale flew up, and the poor soul was condemned to the regions below, and conducted by devils to Eblis' dread abode, there to be tormented with "fire unquenched, unquenchable — around, within his form to dwell." The flame had reached his feet and legs, and was proceeding to envelope his wretched body, when he, sinking into the bottomless pit with but his head above the liquid fire, cried out, "Oh! my patron saint, save me! take compassion on me, and throw into the scale of my good deeds all the lime and stone that I gave to repair the convent." His saint listened to the supplications of the tortured one, and gathering all the materials the monk had collected to build and adorn his monastery, did as he desired, and threw them into the scale of good, which immediately had the effect of overbalancing the evil, and the sinner's soul was taken to Paradise that moment. The moral meant to be conveyed was, how useful to that poor sinner's eternal salvation was his having kept his convent in repair; for had he not bestowed all that lime and stone, his soul would have been to this day consuming in the fires prepared for the Devil and his angels.

Billiards was a game much played by Napoleon and his suite. I had the honour of being instructed in its mysteries by him; but when tired of my

1. Napoleon on board HMS *Bellerophon*; detail from a painting by Sir William Quiller Orchardson. From left to right: Colonel Planat, (a member of Napoleon's suite); Charles Tristan, Comte de Montholon, (secretary, ambassador and long-serving confidante to Napoleon); Pierre Maingaut, (Napoleon's surgeon); Emanuel Auguste Dieudonné Marius Joseph, Marquis Las Cases, (secretary); General Anne Jean Marie René Savary, 1st Duc de Rovigo, (a member of Napoleon's suite); General Charles François Antoine Lallemand, (a member of Napoleon's suite); General Henri Gratien Comte de Bertrand, (Grand Marshal of the Chamber); Emanuel Pons Dieudonné, (later Comte de) Las Cases, (son of the marquis) and Napoleon Bonaparte. Of these, Planat, Maingaut, Savary and Lallemand did <u>not</u> trans-ship to HMS *Northumberland* for the onward journey to St Helena.

2. The scene in Plymouth Sound, August 1815 by John James Chalon. Curious sightseers try to catch a glimpse of Napoleon on HMS *Bellerophon*.

3. The approach to St Helena — a first view that is reported to have made Napoleon's heart sink.

4. One of a series of six aquatints by George Hutchins Bellasis; 'The Roads, St Helena' published November 1815.

5. Another of the Bellasis aquatints; 'Scene Taken from the Castle Terrace, St Helena'.

6. The shore front of James Town looking towards the west. James Town is on the north of the island.

7. A view of James Town from the road leading to the Briars. The church of St James, built in 1774, gained a spire in 1843, but this was demolished in 1980 on the grounds of safety. This view would have been similar to that seen by Napoleon. This is one of a series of views published in 1857 by G. W. Melliss.

8. An older engraving showing the road leading to the Briars, demonstrating the precipitous nature of the island geography.

9. This view from T. E. Fowler's 1863 book on St Helena shows that new buildings had sprung up between the battery and St James's Church. The castelletated front has changed with the insertion of a new battery. This view shows more clearly the second line of defence, with a high wall behind the trees.

10. A view of the Main Street James Town from Fowler's book.

11. Melliss's Views: A view of the upper part of the Main Street of James Town. Note the tricolour on the left-hand side.

12. Admiral Sir George Cockburn, (1772-1853).

13. Governor Mark Wilks, (1760-1831).

Right: 14. Fowler's Views: Plantation House.

Below: 15. An old engraving of Plantation House.

Bottom: 16. Plantation House from the Bellasis aquatints.

Left: 17. Fowler's Views: The Briars.

Centre: 18. Melliss's Views: The Briars.

Below: 19. The Briars from an old engraving.

20. Napoleon meets Jane and Betsy Balcombe. Behind Napoleon stands Las Cases and to the right on the picture, Toby, the Malay slave.

21. William Balcombe, (1779-1829).

22. Jane Balcombe senior.

23. The races on Deadwood Plain, a watercolour by Denzil Ibbetson, (1788-1857), the Commissary in St Helena. Ibbetson sailed on board HMS *Northumberland* and remained on the island throughout Napoelon's captivity.

24. An invented scene by a French artist, with Napoleon dictating to the young Las Cases.

25. A painting of General Henri Gratien Comte de Bertrand, (1773-1844). Count Bertrand remained with Napoleon throughout the captivity. In 1840 he was chosen by the French government, following agreement with the British government to bring Napoleon's remains to France — *le retour des cendres*.

26. An engraving of Emanuel Auguste Dieudonné Marius Joseph Marquis Las Cases, (1776-1842. Las Cases was arrested on 25 November 1816 by Sir Hudson Lowe and deported on 30 December 1816 together with his son.

27. Charles Tristan Comte de Montholon, (1783-1853). Count Montholon remained with Napoleon throughout the captivity.

28. Louis Marchand, (1792-1876). Marchand was First Valet to Napoleon at Longwood and executor to his will. His mother was nurse to Napleon's son, the King of Rome. He remained throughout the captivity and returned in 1840 for the exhumation and *le retour des cendres*.

29. The upper James Town valley.

30. The modern road at the upper James Town valley.

31. A current view of the site of the Briars. The original bungalow was destroyed by termites and demolished. In the later nineteenth century the site was the property of Solomon and Cole, the main island traders. It became a French domain following the purchase and donation by Dame Mabel Brooke, the grand-niece of Betsy, in 1957.

32. The mountainous track close to the Briars.

33. A continuation of a track close to the Briars.

34. An island view close to High Ridge.

35. A general view from High Ridge.

36. A view towards Sandy Bay.

37. Diana's Peak.

38. Another view from High Ridge.

39. Pastoral St Helena.

40. The current view from Longwood. The garden would have looked very different in 1820.

41. A view from General Bertrand's cottage, close to Longwood.

42. Melliss's Views: General Bertrand's cottage. Bertrand lived here with his Irish-born wife, Frances, née Dillon, the daughter of General Arthur Dillon, an Irish refugee. Their children (of whom Napoleon was very fond) were Napoleon, Henri, Hortense and Arthur. The latter was born on the island.

43. An engraving of Longwood, date unknown. The illustration is something of a mystery as it shows a wooden outbuilding and a masonry wall not shown on other illustrations. It appears in Jacques Bainville's *Napoleon*, 1932. A building looking like a watchtower is to the left, apparently with a flag flying. Longwood appears in a dilapidated state and it may be mid-nineteenth century when the building was used as a granary.

44. A wash illustration of Longwood from Julian Park's *Count Balmain*, 1928. This is presumably an early twentieth-century illustration with the building now under French protection. The wooden building has been removed and the property looks in much better condition.

45. Napoleon and Betsy, an imaginary French illustration — *composition de fantaisie*. It appears as if Napoleon is about to give Betsy his gift of a snuff box.

46. Napoleon in his garden. Towards the end when he threw his enthusiasm into his garden, he abandoned his bicorn cocked hat with cockade, and adopted a straw hat and a flannel suit.

47. An illustration, apparently drawn from life and dated 1820 from Philippe Gonnard, *The Exile of St Helena*, 1909.

48. Napoleon gardening at Longwood, another imaginary French illustration.

49. Napoleon in 1818, a watercolour painted from life and said to be a very good likeness. It was painted by Lt.-Colonel Basil Jackson of the Staff Corps in St Helena. This was given by the artist to the Countess of Bertrand.

50. Napoleon in 1820 from a drawing made by Captain Henry Duncan Dodgin of the 66th Regiment.

51. The Friar Rock in Friars Valley, from the G. H. Bellasis 'Views'.

52. Lot's Column, Friar Land and Sandy Bay, from the G. H. Bellasis 'Views'.

53. Lieutenant-General Sir Hudson Lowe, (1769-1844).

54. Napoleon arguing at Longwood, with Sir Hudson Lowe; another imaginary French illustration.

55. Major Charles Robert George Hodson, (1779-1858); of the St Helena Regiment, and Judge Advocate.

56. Major Gideon Gorrequer, (1781-1841); Aide-de-Camp and Acting Military Secretary to Sir Hudson Lowe.

57. John Stokoe, (1775-1852); Surgeon to the *Conqueror*. Stokoe was summoned to attend Napoleon 17 January 1819 and over the next four days paid five visits incurring the displeasure of Lowe.

58. Barry Edward O'Meara, (1782-1836); Medical Attendant to Napoleon until 25 July 1818 when Lowe caused him to be removed.

59. A portrait of Napoleon in the last phase of his life.

60. Archibald Arnott M.D., (1771-1855); Surgeon to the 20ᵗʰ Foot Regiment. Arnott had excellent relations with Napoleon who gave him a gold snuff box. He attended Napoleon in his last days and attended the post-mortem.

61. Thomas Shortt, (1788-1843); Principal Medical Officer in St Helena. He arrived at the island in December 1820 and was consulted on Napoleon's illness, He attended the post-mortem.

62. Laura Wilks, (1797-1888); daughter of the Governor, Mark Wilks. Laura was a friend to Betsy and Jane; she was received by Napoleon on several occasions and he remarked on her beauty. She left the island with her father and mother on 20 April 1816.

Above: 63. A watercolour painting presumably by Louis Marchand, Napoleon's valet. This painting was offered to Napoleon 1 January 1820 and appears to be reasonably faithful depiction of the garden Napoleon created. At the far back of the garden is the tall turf wall Napoleon had built. Given Sir Hudson Lowe's antagonism, it is somewhat surprising that he was allowed to get away with it.

Below: 64. A watercolour by Denzil Ibbetson. He remained on the island until June 1823, so presumably this painting was executed between May 1821 and June 1823. It attributes the various chambers of the house and adds: 'the House in which Napoleon died . . . which is now a granary'. In the turf wall is the spy hole cut for Napoleon to use for his telescope.

65. Napoleon on his death bed by Denzil Ibbetson. Napoleon died of a stomach ulcer with cancerous complications.

66. The dimensions of Napoleon's head recorded by Denzil Ibbetson.

Right: 67. Napoleon's death mask. Great problems were encountered by this; a first mask was only partly successful due to faulty plaster. A second mask was successful when quality plaster was sourced, but by that time bodily decomposition had set it in.

68. The death chamber at Longwood.

Above: 69. Napoleon's funeral,
21 May 1821.

Centre top: 70. Melliss's Views: The
tomb of Napoleon.

Centre bottom: 71. Fowler's Views:
The tomb valley and the road to
Longwood.

Below: 72. *Le retour des cendres*
from the St Helena to France and
their burial in the Hôtel des Invalides
in Paris in 1840, on the initiative
of Adolphe Thiers and King Louis-
Philippe. On 10 May 1840 François
Guizot, then French ambassador in
London, submitted an official request
to the British government, which was
immediately approved according to
the promise made in 1822. By the light
of torches, British soldiers exhumed
the body on 14 October 1840.

73. A sketch of Betsy in early adult life.

74. A painting of Betsy *c.* 1822.

75. An engraving of Betsy —
Mrs Abell, in 1844.

76. A miniature of Betsy's daughter, Jane
Elizabeth Balcombe Abell, (1827-1892).

Above 77. A gold and tortoise-shell box: the Montholons' wedding gift to Betsy, 1822.

Left 78. Dame Mabel Brookes, (1890-1975), Betsy's grand-niece, at the gates of the Briars, 1957.

79. Napoleon's 40-inch waist breeches.

80. A lock of Napoleon's hair that had been in the possession of Denzil Ibbetson.

lesson, my amusement consisted in aiming the balls at his fingers, and I was never more pleased than when I succeeded in making him cry out. One day our pass from Sir Hudson Lowe only specified a visit to General Bertrand, but my anxiety to see Napoleon, caused me to break through the rule laid down, and the consequences of my imprudence were nearly proving very serious, as my father *all but* lost the appointment he then held under government. I had caught sight of the emperor in his favourite billiard-room, and not being able to resist having a game with him, I listened to no remonstrance, but bounded off, leaving my father in dismay at the consequences likely to ensue. Instead of my anticipated game of throwing about the balls, I was requested to read a book, by Dr Warden, the surgeon of the *Northumberland*, that had just come out. It was in English, and I had the task of wading through several chapters, and making it as intelligible as my ungrammatical French permitted. Napoleon was much pleased with Dr Warden's book, and said, "his work was a very true one." I finished reading it to him whilst we remained with Madame Bertrand.

In the cool of the evening we used to have chairs brought out and placed on the lawn leading to the billiard-room, under the gum-wood trees, and the Countesses Bertrand and Montholon, with their husbands and children, my sister and myself, would remain for hours after sunset listening to the thousand crickets with which the ground at Longwood seemed alive. The moonlight nights were remarkably beautiful at St Helena; the blue of the sky so deep and clear, that it would be difficult to imagine any scene more solemn and imposing than the appearance presented by the landscape on such occasions. Either the stars shine brighter in that firmament, and the moon seems fuller and more lustrous, or it may be that the recollection of those joyous days had no cloud to dim their radiance. It was on one of these splendid starry nights, and at the time we were on a visit to Madame Bertrand, that the party was grouped about, some seated on the steps of the billiard-room, others in the garden enjoying the cool refreshing breeze. The day had been one of the most sultry ever experienced within the recollection of the oldest inhabitant of St Helena. Suddenly we heard a lumbering heavy noise, as if loaded wagons were rumbling over the ground immediately under us. Those seated near the billiard room sprang up aghast, thinking the house was falling about their ears. Dr O'Meara and Major Blakeney,[59] who was appointed captain of the guard at Longwood, rushed immediately from their rooms, expecting to find the ladies half dead with fear. All the household, some of whom were in bed, ran out in the greatest alarm; some were gazing up at the sky, others looking stupified with wonder and amazement as to what had caused such a commotion. Little Tristan Montholon, who had some time previously retired to rest, came screaming to his mother, declaring that somebody had been trying to throw him out of bed. The cause of our terror proved to be an earthquake, the only one remembered to have occurred at St Helena for nearly a century.[60] The horror this event occasioned us all, can only be conceived by those who are acquainted with the island; more especially was the alarm felt by those whose friends and relatives were residing in any of the valleys, so narrow and wedge-like in their form, and flanked, as they generally were, by tremendous overhanging precipices, at the summit of which enormous loose rocks threatened continual destruction to those who were beneath. It was observed at the time, that had the shocks been lateral, instead of perpendicular, those who resided in the valleys must have been destroyed by the vast boulders of stone which would have fallen from the mountains above. Napoleon had retired to bed, and it was not till the next morning that we saw him. He asked us if we had been frightened by the *tremblement de terre* on the previous evening, observing that I looked pale and quiet. He mentioned to General Bertrand that he at first thought the *Conqueror*, a 74 lying in the harbour,[61] had blown up, and that the great powder magazine had exploded, but on feeling the third shock he perceived it to be an earthquake. It lasted from 16 to 18 seconds. Many people fancied the rumbling noise they at first heard to be thunder, but when it was remembered that such a phenomenon as thunder was never heard, nor had lightning ever been seen since the discovery of St Helena, that idea was abandoned. Thunder and lightning have never been known to disturb the harmony of the climate. To account for this, it is said that the electric fluid is attracted by a high and conical-shaped mountain, called Diana's Peak, and conducted by it into the sea. I was too much alarmed after the occurrence of the earthquake to go to bed for many nights.

Seeing me one day unusually low-spirited, Napoleon inquired what could possibly have happened to drive away the dimples from my usually *riant* face. "Has any one run away with a favourite *proté da bal*, or is the pet black nurse, old Sarah, dead! What can have occurred?" I told him it was neither one thing nor the other, but simply that our kind lady governess, Mrs Wilks,[62] had left the island, and such demonstrations of grief had never before been seen at St Helena. She was so beloved, people of all ranks and ages crowded to the castle to say, "God bless you, and a safe and happy voyage home." Not a dry eye was to be seen amongst the crowd then collected; that leave-taking of our much loved and respected governor and his family resembled more a funeral than a levee; so sad and solemn was every face. I fancy I can see them now, following the party to the beach as they embarked in the barge that conducted them on board the *Havannah*; and when the noble frigate spread her canvas to the swelling breeze that bore from the little rock those who had contributed so much to the happiness of its gratefully impressed inhabitants, groups of sorrow-stricken ladies were seen wandering under the pepul trees of the Sisters' Walk watching the vessel as she lessened from their tearful gaze, bearing on board a family who had rendered themselves so popular by their urbanity and kindness, which is even remembered to this day. I recounted the scene we had witnessed (and suffered with the rest) to the emperor; he was quite interested in the recital, and regretted much not having been acquainted with the lady governess, as she must have been so very amiable.

Napoleon's hour for rising was uncertain; though generally early, it much depended on the rest he took during the day, or the sultry state of the weather; occasionally he would sleep for an hour or two on the bench under our trellised grape walk at the "Briars," and when he awoke refreshed, would write or dictate away for hours together. Sometimes he would diversify his occupation by riding round our lawn on his beautiful black horse "Hope." The name pleased him; it was the first he had ridden on the island, and he liked the augury. After his long *day* sleeps he would court the drowsy god at night by desiring Marchand to read to him until the "sweet restorer, nature's soft nurse," came to his aid. Frequently, when the nights were illumined by the splendid tropical moon, would he rise at three o'clock, and saunter down to the garden long before old Toby, the slave, had slept off his first nap, and there he would regale himself with an early breakfast of delicious fruits with which our garden abounded. Our old Malay was so fond of the man Bony, as he designated the emperor, that he always placed the garden key where Napoleon's fingers could reach it under the wicket. No one else was ever favoured in the like manner, but he had completely fascinated and won the old man's heart, and Napoleon looked upon Toby with a kind of romantic interest, as one who had been cruelly wronged in his youthful career. After these early risings, he generally fasted until eleven, when he would breakfast *à la fourchette* with his suite; he usually ate very fast, but did not admire highly seasoned dishes. He preferred a roasted leg of mutton to any other English joint, and I have often seen him take the knuckle in his hand and pare off all the brown part of it.

Napoleon had some very beautiful seals and rare coins, from which he good-naturedly employed himself in taking off impressions in sealing-wax. Whilst he was thus engaged, I once mischievously jogged his elbow, and caused him to drop the hot wax on his fingers. It was very painful, and raised a large blister; but he was so very good-natured about it, that I told him I was quite sorry for what I had done; whereas, had he been cross, I should have rejoiced.

CHAPTER XV

It was not long after Napoleon had been at Longwood, that chance took him in one of his rides to a romantic glen named "The Friar's Valley," a wildly picturesque spot, so called from the peculiar formation of a huge rock fashioned by nature's hand into the figure of a monk with his cowl thrown back, dressed in flowing robes, with a rosary at his side. He forms a peculiar feature in the grotesque scenery with which great part of the island abounds; that immediately around it, consisting of stupendous sterile rocks, detached by deep and frightful ravines, some rising perpendicularly many hundred feet; and here and there are seen bare masses of stone towering aloft, with flowering aloes bursting forth from fissures in their iron coloured sides. I have endeavoured to convey, in the annexed sketch, some faint idea of this romantic though, desolate looking valley. Napoleon had heard of the legend connected with it, and asked me if I had ever seen the "Will-o'-the-Wisp," which he was told lighted the old friar's lantern. I said I had been often frightened by it, for when quite a little child, my mother, thinking the air on the mountains purer than that of St James's Valley, generally sent me thither under the care of an old negro nurse, who resided in a little cottage directly overlooking the vale. Oftentimes would she threaten, if I did not repeat my letters correctly, to give me to the monk, who would carry me off in his lantern.

I perfectly recollect how heartily the emperor laughed at my describing the tricks I played old Sarah. I had a box of letters, which it was her daily duty to see me arrange and place in alphabetical order: my great fun was to turn them topsy-turvy, at the same time keeping them quite straight. When I placed them *properly*, I arranged them unevenly; but the dear old nurse, who did not understand a letter in her alphabet, was certain to commend me for the *neat* arrangement I had effected; but I was threatened with the friar when my lesson presented an untidy appearance, however right it might be.

The story attached to the valley was this. The place where the friar now stands, was supposed once to have been the site of a Roman Catholic chapel, adjoining which was the residence of the officiating priest, a monk of the Franciscan order, who was considered an example of Christian piety and humility, his life being passed in the performance of acts of charity and benevolence, such as attending the sick, relieving the oppressed; and often did he interpose his charitable interference between the severe taskmaster and his wretched slaves, when the latter were condemned for some trifling offence to undergo fearful mutilations or the cruel lash. Thus in acts of piety this man of God pursued his way, blessing and blessed, till his senses became enthralled by the surpassing beauty of a mountain nymph, who dwelt in a cottage not far removed from the friar's lonely habitation. It was in one of his rambles in search of some object of charity that his eyes first encountered this lovely daughter of the Atlantic isle, tending a herd of her father's mountain goats; they had strayed so far that she had vainly tried to collect them, and was returning tired and sad to her dwelling, when, encountering the monk, she humbly told her tale, and asked his assistance. It was readily accorded, for who could resist such an appeal, enhanced by so much beauty? The scattered flock was reunited, and the young girl, gracefully acknowledging his service, with a light heart returned to her home. It would have been well for the good father had that interview been the last, but fate ordained it otherwise. Again and again he sought her mountain cot, pouring into the maiden's ear his tale of love and adoration, and finally besought her to be his bride. She promised, but on one condition only, to listen to his suit — he must renounce his creed, and become of her faith: upon these terms alone would she consent, and until he had resolved thus to prove his devotion, must not hope to see her again. The struggle was a fearful one in the breast of the monk; but love triumphed in the end: he forsook the faith of his fathers, broke his vows, and became a renegade. In due course of time the wedding-day was fixed: the ceremony was to be performed in that very chapel which had so often re-echoed the apostate's pious prayers for his suffering flock, and the bride, accompanied by her attendant maidens, approached the altar. The service was read, and just as the bridegroom was clasping the hand of his beloved, a fearful crash resounded, the rock was rent asunder, and every vestige of the chapel, and of those it contained, for ever disappeared. In its place stands the gaunt image of the grim friar, — an example and a sad warning to those who suffer their evil passions to prevail over their better judgment.

I remember one morning seeing the emperor much moved; he had been exhibiting a marble bust of the King of Rome, which had been sent to him by the Empress Marie Louise. He took us into his bedroom to inspect them, and we were loud in our praises of the beauty of the child who could have furnished the sculptor with so attractive a subject for his classical art. Napoleon gazed on it with proud satisfaction, and was evidently much delighted at our warm encomiums upon its loveliness. My mother told him he ought indeed to exult at being the father of such a beautiful creature as that boy must be. Smiles seemed to light up his face, and my mother often said, she never saw a countenance at the time so interestingly expressive of parental fondness. The bust of the young Napoleon was the size of life, exquisitely chiselled in white marble; and on it was inscribed "Napoleon Francois Charles Joseph," etc., it bore the decoration of the Grand Cross of the Legion of Honour. It was sent mysteriously to Napoleon, and arrived in charge of a sailor, who had received it through the orders of Marie Louise: the sculptor resided at Leghorn, and the empress had it conveyed to the gunner of a ship bound for St Helena, (it was said,) as a silent token of her regard and unchanged affection for the ex-emperor. When we had seen and admired this treasure, Madame Bertrand invited us to accompany her, and be charmed by the exhibition of a variety of presents from Lady Holland, which had been sent out and had arrived only a few days before. They offered a rich feast to my eyes; such an assemblage of beautiful trinkets I had never beheld, and I viewed them again and again in an ecstasy of delight.

Lady Holland was very kind to Mesdames Bertrand and Montholon, especially to the former; and many were the grateful prayers I have heard her offer for the happiness of that excellent lady, who evinced such true charity in displaying so many considerate attentions, which could not but be highly appreciated under such circumstances. Napoleon, when speaking of her ladyship, always called her "La bonne Lady Holland," and expressed himself very grateful for her kindness and attention to him, when abandoned by the world in that desolate island. He remarked, that all the members of the family of the great Fox abounded in liberal and generous sentiments. In speaking of that statesman he used to say,[64] "He was sincere and honest in his intentions, and had he lived, England would not have been desolated by war; he was the only minister who knew the interests of his country." He said he was received with a kind of triumph in every city of the French empire, and *fêted* and welcomed by all its inhabitants. Every town he visited seemed to vie with the other which should offer him the greatest honours. He related a circumstance which, he said, must have made a gratifying impression on the mind of that great man. One day Fox visited St Cloud. The private apartments of the palace there were never shown, being exclusively kept for the use of the emperor; however, by some accident the minister and Mrs Fox opened one of the doors of the sanctum, and entered; there they beheld statues of the great men of all times and nations — Sydney, Hampden, Washington, Cicero, Lord Chatham, and amongst the rest his own, which was instantly recognised by his lady, who exclaimed, "My dear, this is yours." This little incident, though trifling, procured him great attentions, and spread directly through Paris.

CHAPTER XVI

I recollect being at Longwood one beautiful day; the atmosphere had that peculiar lightness and brilliancy which in a great measure constituted the charm of the climate of St Helena. The sea lay glistening in the sun like a sheet of quicksilver, the little merry waves bursting in sparkling foam at the foot of the stupendous rocks, and the exquisite soft verdure immediately surrounding Longwood formed a very pleasing contrast to the stern features of the rest of the island. It was one of those days in which the *past* and the *future* are alike disregarded; anxious thought is suspended for a moment, and the present alone is felt and enjoyed. I remember bounding up to St Dennis[65] and asking for Napoleon; my joyousness was somewhat damped by the gravity with which he replied, that the emperor was watching the approach of the *Conqueror*, then coming in, bearing the flag of Admiral Plampin.[66] "You will find him," he said, "near Madame Bertrand's, but he is in no mood for badinage today, Mademoiselle." Notwithstanding this check, I proceeded towards the cottage, and in a moment the whole tone of my mind was changed from gaiety to sadness. Young as I was, I could not help being strongly impressed by the intense melancholy of his expression; "the ashes of a thousand thoughts were on his brow;"[67] he was standing with General Bertrand, his eyes bent sadly on the 74, which was yet but a speck in the line of the horizon. The magnificent ship soon grew upon our sight, as, beating up to windward, silently yet proudly she pursued her brave career. "Sailing amid the loneliness, like a thing endowed with heart and mind," she seemed the very impersonation of majesty! Byron thought the ocean, with a single vessel moving over it, the most poetical object in nature; perhaps its utter loneliness is the cause. The thought has since occurred to me, that Napoleon might then have gazed upon that ship as typical of his own fortunes, so lordly, yet mastered, and impelled by some unseen resistless power towards that wild shore destined to be the tomb of all his daring hopes and mad ambition. Such spirits are undoubtedly sent into the world by an omniscient Providence for a beneficent and merciful purpose; their fiery course is run; they would still urge on, but their headlong rashness may be made the instrument of their ruin; and the stern hand of death arrest them before they have tasted of that earthly glory for which they toiled; their deeds, however, still live, and become often benefits to mankind, though springing from an evil source.

The emperor, after a long silence, commented on the beautiful management of the vessel. "The English are kings upon the sea," he said, and then, smiling somewhat sarcastically, added, "I wonder what they think of our beautiful island; they cannot be much elated by the sight of my gigantic prison walls!" His natural prejudice against the island rendered him blind to the many beauties with which it abounded; he beheld all with a jaundiced eye: thus ever do our views of life take their colouring from our feelings and the nature of the circumstances in which we are placed. "Our eyes see all around in gloom with hues of their own, fresh borrowed from the heart." He would frequently rail at the island in no measured language; I always defended it in proportionate terms of praise. Sometimes he laughed at my impertinence, and at others he would pinch my ear, and ask me how I could possibly dare to have an opinion on the subject.

The emperor had that great charm in social life, of being amused and interested in matters of trifling import. It seems to me to be an attribute of his countrymen, from which, no doubt, they derive that vivacity and *talent de société* generally possessed by them, but which, from our inherent reserve and national shyness, would sit awkwardly on us, English. It would be something like the statue of Hercules in the National Gallery stepping from his pedestal and taking Cerito's place in the "Pas de l'Ombre." Napoleon was very fond of extracting from me my little store of knowledge, acquired from, I fear, rather desultory reading. However, being fond of books, and having a retentive memory, I could apparently chain his interest for some hours. "Now, Mademoiselle Betsee," he would say, "I hope you have been goot child and learnt all your lesson;" which he said purposely to annoy me, as I was anxious to be thought full grown, and, like most young ladies of my age, scorned the idea of being called a child, deeming myself fully competent to embark upon the troublous sea of life, and to battle with its storms without the rudder of experience. He was much interested in a favourite study of mine, namely, the account of the discovery and colonization of St Helena by the Portuguese, and he would listen attentively while I repeated it, for I had it almost by heart.

My young brother, Alexander, had a pet goat, of which he was very fond, and the animal used to draw him about in a little carriage. One day Napoleon

had given him a little box, made by Piron, full of *bon-bons*: when my brother
had eaten all his sugar-plums, and was grieving over his exhausted store,
he unluckily chanced to espy a pill-box, which, with other medicines, had
been inadvertently placed on a bench in the garden; he carefully put some
of its contents into his *bonbonniére*, and gravely walking up to the emperor,
presented it. Napoleon, always good-natured to the child, and supposing
them to be sugar-plums, helped himself to one, and began eating it. I need
not say how soon it was ejected, and what coughing and nausea ensued,
when my little brother's mischievous trick was divulged, and it was found
that pills of a very unpalatable nature had been offered to and swallowed
by the emperor. The poor little fellow got soundly whipped by my father,
to whom his naughty conduct had been made known by Las Cases, who
witnessed the joke and immediately reported it; he knew my father to be too
severe a disciplinarian to overlook even a trifling fault.

My father had been suffering from a very violent attack of gout, which
prevented his riding to Longwood, as was his daily habit. When he saw
Napoleon after his recovery, the emperor began laughing at him, and told
him, if he sat a shorter time after dinner, he would have fewer attacks of
gout. He asked him what remedies he had resorted to to be cured. My father
replied, he had taken "Eau medicinale," upon which Napoleon laughingly
remarked, had he drank more pure water and less wine he might have
dispensed with the *eau medicinale*. He told him he was too young to want
physic, as remedies ought only to be resorted to by the old. In speaking
of his own abstemious habits, he observed that he drank very little wine;
however, the little he did drink was absolutely taken medicinally, and he
always found himself better after it, feeling convinced that if he left it off,
he should soon become ill. One of his principal specifics was a warm salt
water bath. Dr O'Meara told us that having recommended Napoleon a dose
of medicine, soon after he came to St Helena, he answered him by a slap
in the face, and told him if he were not better on the morrow, he should
have recourse to his own remedy — abstinence and a bath. He was very
fond of asking anatomical questions, and often fancied he had disease of the
heart, and made O'Meara count its pulsations. He constantly complained
of illness from the exposed situation of Longwood, the wind continually
beating in his face, or the sun scorching his brain; he used to observe, when
at the Briars, that he never suffered any ailment, for there he had shady
and sheltered walks. Certainly Longwood was very bleak, and scarcely any
vegetables would grow upon it, except a kind of coarse cow-grass, which
even horses refuse.

A long interval frequently elapsed between our visits to the emperor. A few months previously to our leaving St Helena he had been very ill, and from Dr O'Meara's account we feared he might never rally from the state of prostration of mind and body into which he had sunk. He was obstinate in refusing to take exercise, disliking the strict watch kept over him on the occasion of his walking abroad; and he declared he would rather die at once than use the only means recommended of alleviating his disorder. Dr O'Meara entreated permission to call in a brother surgeon, that in the event of his complaint continuing obstinate, blame might not be attached to him for trusting solely to his own opinion. I recollect hearing Dr O'Meara repeat the emperor's reply, which was to this effect; "that if all the physicians in the universe were collected, they would but repeat what *you* have already advised me — to take constant exercise on horseback. I am well aware of the truth of what you say, but were I to call in Mr ——, it would be but like sending a physician to a starving man, instead of giving him a loaf of bread. I have no objection to your making known to him my state of health, if it be any satisfaction to you; but I know that he will say — *exercise*. As long as this strict surveillance is enforced I will never stir out." It was in vain, Dr O'Meara again and again urged the subject, his invariable reply was, "Would you have me render myself liable to be stopped and insulted by the sentries surrounding my house, as Madame Bertrand was some days ago?" It would have made a fine caricature in the London print shops, — Napoleon Bonaparte stopped at the gate by a sentinel charging him with fixed bayonet. How the Londoners would have laughed! The only one of his suite who appeared careless of these restrictions was General Gourgaud; he had been stopped, Napoleon observed, fifty times. Once, when at the Briars, he said, he had been treated rather unceremoniously by a sentry, and complaints being made to the Admiral, that officer was really displeased about it, and took every precaution to prevent a recurrence of such annoyance.

When we saw Napoleon after this illness, the havoc and change it had made in his appearance was sad to look upon. His face was literally the colour of yellow wax, and his cheeks had fallen in pouches on either side his face. His ankles were so swollen that the flesh literally hung over his shoes; he was so weak, that without resting one hand on a table near him, and the other on the shoulder of an attendant, he could not have stood. I was so grieved at seeing him in such a pitiable state, that my eyes overflowed with tears, and I could with difficulty forbear sobbing aloud. He saw how shocked we were, and tried to make light of it, saying, he was sure the good O'Meara would soon cure him; but my mother observed, when we had left, that death was stamped on every feature. He, however, rallied from this attack, to pass nearly three more years in hopeless misery; for it became more evident to him that the anticipation in which he indulged (on first coming to St Helena) of quitting the island, became fainter as health declined, and time wore on.

The emperor expressed much curiosity to be introduced to a Mr Manning who had arrived at St Helena on his voyage to England from China,[68] which country he had visited after exploring the unknown, and at that time, untravelled, kingdom of Tibet. Napoleon said he had a great curiosity to hear something relating to their mode of worshipping the Grand Lama, as he was induced to believe most of the accounts he had read and heard of it were fabulous. I described the impression Mr Manning had made on me by his imposing appearance; his dress was like that of a Mandarin, and he wore a long black beard which reached to his waist. He had, during the war, been a prisoner in France, and had been treated with great clemency by Napoleon; thus was each party anxious to see the other. Mr Manning had brought many very curious presents for Napoleon, which he had collected in his travels. He obtained a pass to see the emperor; he said he had been presented to the Lama, who was a very intelligent boy of seven years old; that he had gone through the same forms as the other worshippers who were admitted to the celestial presence. Napoleon asked him if he were not afraid of being seized as a spy. The traveller did not seem pleased that the emperor should have thought that his appearance could have conveyed such an impression; but he laughingly pointed to his beard and dress, and seemed much diverted with his interview. He could not think how they, jealous as they were in their religious rites, should have admitted an unbeliever into their sacred temple, and have permitted him to approach the Lama. Mr Manning said he honoured and respected all religions, as did Napoleon.

The emperor wished to know if he had passed for an Englishman, as the shape of his nose was too good for a Tartar. Mr Manning replied, that he had been taken for a Hindoo, which, from the regularity of his features and fine eyes, might easily have been the case. Napoleon told him that travellers were privileged to tell marvellous stories, and he hoped he was not doing so in relating the wonders of Tibet. He wanted to know if it were true that the revenues of the Grand Lama were derived from the gifts of the multitudes that daily flocked from all parts to worship at his shrine, as well as from priestly extortion. Manning told the emperor it was quite true, and complimented him upon being as well informed as the traveller himself. The Lama was subject to the Chinese; he never married, neither did his priest; the body into which, according to their belief, the spirit passed, was found out by the priests from certain signs. Napoleon's conference with the traveller lasted some time; he asked a thousand questions respecting the Chinese, their language, customs, etc. When the interview was concluded, he observed it had given him greater pleasure than he had experienced for many long months.

CHAPTER XVII

Upon one occasion, Sir George Bingham[69] gave a grand ball to all the people on the island, as a sort of return for civilities shown to him and his officers of the 53rd regiment. It was the prettiest thing of the kind and the best one I ever remember either before or since; and as the scene of revel was close to Longwood, we were told the emperor had the curiosity to take a peep at it *incog*. I verily believe he had, from the faithful and animated detail he entered into respecting it the next day, and his criticisms upon dancing, dress, etc. The first attempt at waltzing was made on that occasion in the Saraband, and he took off a certain young lady's graceless movements so inimitably, that we felt sure he had indulged himself with a peep.

Sir G. Cockburn had a beautiful dog of the Newfoundland breed, which was a great favourite, both from its beauty and docility. It was very fond of accompanying its noble master whenever he honoured the Briars with a visit, for the place abounded with ponds and rivulets, in which Tom Pipes delighted to swim and cool himself after following at the horses' heels up the mountain, under a sultry tropical sun. One time, as Napoleon was engaged making notes in the garden of the Briars, close to a large pond full of gold and silver fish, I called the dog to have a gambol and refresh himself with a bath, well knowing his custom was to shake his huge sides after ducking, and then woe betide the person nearest him whilst this operation was performing, they were sure to have their clothes completely saturated. Such was now the case; for Pipes enjoyed his bath immensely, and dived and ducked about, much to the consternation of the gold and silver fish. When he thought he had had enough, he scrambled up the bank, took his place by the emperor's side, who was so much absorbed by his employment as to be unaware of the shower bath in store for him, and it was not until a vigorous shake of the dog, and a plentiful besprinkling all over dress and person, that he found out the mischief of which I had been the cause. The paper on which he had written was spoiled, and he presented a very deplorable figure himself. It was impossible to help laughing, although he was very angry, for

Tom Pipes would not go away; he had been a shipmate of Napoleon's on board the *Northumberland*, and was so glad to see him again, that he kept jumping on him with his wet paws, thereby adding mud to wet and dust.

One morning as we were walking, or rather scrambling, among the rocks that close in the waterfall near the Briars, we espied something hanging over the ledge of a rock above us which had the appearance of a soldier in his uniform: the height was so great, and the precipice so perpendicular, that it was an utter impossibility for us to attempt scaling it to ascertain what it could be; but still it looked so strange, and the position of the man (if man it were) so perilous, that we determined on returning to the cottage to send forth someone of bolder heart and steadier nerves than our party possessed, who might throw a light upon the mysterious occupant of the rocky ledge. On our way, we encountered Count Las Cases and the emperor, whose curiosity had also been directed to the object which had excited our attention; he had seen it from his pavilion, and was reconnoitring it with his little spy-glass, the same with which he viewed the battle of Waterloo. We asked him what he thought it could be; he looked grave, and replied, we had better return to the house and remain there for a time, as we might probably be shocked at a scene which he doubted not would soon present itself. He had discovered, by the aid of his glass, that the object which had raised our curiosity, was the corpse of a soldier, who must have met his death by some dreadful accident; his conjecture was soon ascertained to be too true. A soldier had obtained leave of absence the night before for a few hours, and was to have been back by sunset. He outstayed his leave, beguiling time with some old comrades, and had perhaps indulged too freely at the shrine of Bacchus. But be that as it may, on finding he had exceeded his time, and being well aware of the severe discipline necessarily maintained at this time on the island, he had tried to reach his barrack by a short cut, missed his footing, and was precipitated over the ledge, falling from a height of at least one hundred feet. We were all in a state of the most painful excitement during the ceremony of the coroner's inquest which was held on the dead man. I recollect Napoleon did not lose that occasion of hinting to my father, that if the poor soldier had sat less time after dinner he probably would not have met with so dreadful a fate.

About that time there was quite a chapter of tragical accidents, one of which has flashed on my mind. My young brother had a kind of tutor, *faute de mieux*,[70] a curious character, whose name was Huff; he had been an inhabitant of the island I believe at that time nearly half a century. This old man, since the arrival of Napoleon, had taken many strange fancies into his brain; among others, that he was destined to restore the fallen hero to his pristine glory, and that he could at any time free him from thraldom. All argument with this old man upon the folly of his ravings was useless; he still persisted in it, and it soon became evident that old Huff was mad, and, though strictly watched, he found an opportunity one fatal morning to destroy himself. An inquest was held on him, *felo de se* returned as verdict, (for there was much method evinced in his madness,) and his body was ordered to be interred in the spot where three crossroads met. The nearest to the scene where the act was committed was the road leading to the Briars, and there they buried the old man.

I had amongst many other follies a terror of ghosts, and this weakness was well known to the emperor, who, for a considerable time after the suicide of poor Huff, used to frighten me nearly into fits. Every night, just before my hour of retiring to my room, he would call out, "Miss Betsee, ole Huff, ole Huff:" The misery of those nights I shall never forget; I used generally to fly out of my bed during the night, and scramble into my mother's room, and remain there till morning's light dispelled the terrors of darkness.

One evening, when my mother, my sister and myself were quietly sitting in the porch of the cottage, enjoying the coolness of the night breeze, suddenly we heard a noise, and turning round beheld a figure in white — how I screamed. We were then greeted with a low gruff laugh, which my mother instantly knew to be the emperor's. She turned the white covering, and underneath appeared the black visage of a little servant of ours, whom Napoleon had instigated to frighten Miss Betsee, while he was himself a spectator of the effect of his trick. This pleasantry of Napoleon's gave rise soon after to a ghost scene, which was enacted to the life by one of our runaway slaves, of the name of Alley; he had been missing for many weeks, and had eluded all search. Pigs, poultry, bread, all the contents of the larder nightly disappeared, no one knew how; but the servants affirmed that a figure in white was seen hovering around the valley, and skipping from rock to rock; they were so alarmed, none would venture out singly. Days and weeks went on, Napoleon's cook complaining, in common with ours, of depredations committed on his *cuisine*; and not having the benefit of a market to replace the loss, it was a matter of no small annoyance. I firmly believed it to be Huff's ghost, and became quite ill from sleepless nights, being literally afraid to close my eyes. At length, after repeated unsuccessful watching, my father and some friends saw a figure stealing along the valley which led towards the house; they watched it uninterruptedly, until it appeared within hail, and upon receiving no answer to their challenge, they fired in the direction. A scream soon told the effect of their shot. Hastening to the spot, they beheld a negro slave, whom they discovered to be the runaway Alley. The poor boy was much hurt, though not mortally. When daylight came they repaired to his haunt, which was the most ingeniously contrived cave, nature ever formed; imperceptible until you came close to it, the entrance being low, and covered by a sheltering rock. There he had lived for weeks, close to his master, and had nightly prowled about, lightening our larders, and robbing the hen roosts.

Napoleon entered the cave with us, and seemed much diverted at the piles of bones collected and neatly arranged by the slave, after he had disposed of their various integuments. He said it reminded him of one of the catacombs in Paris.

I recollect exhibiting to Napoleon a caricature of him in the act of climbing a ladder, each step he ascended represented some vanquished country; at length he was seated astride upon the world. It was a famous toy, and by a dexterous trick Napoleon appeared on the contrary side tumbling down head over heels, and after a perilous descent, alighting on St Helena. I ought not to have shown him this burlesque on his misfortunes, but at that time I was guilty of every description of mad action, though without any intention of being unkind; still I fear they were often deeply felt. My father, of whom I always stood in awe, heard of my rudeness, and desired me to consider myself under arrest for at least a week, and I was transferred from the drawing-room to a dark cellar, and there left to solitude and repentance. I did not soon forget that punishment, for the excavation swarmed with rats, that leaped about me on all sides. I was half dead with horror, and should most certainly have been devoured alive by the vermin, had I not in despair seized a bottle of wine, and dashed it amongst my assailants; finding that I succeeded in occasioning a momentary panic, I continued to diminish the pile of claret near me, and kept my enemies at bay. As the first faint light of morning dawned through my prison bars, I was startled to perceive what my victory would cost my father, for I was surrounded by heaps of broken bottles, and rivulets of wine, and either from exhaustion, or the exhalation from the saturated ground of the cellar, I was found by the slave who brought me my breakfast in the morning, in a state of stupor from which I was with difficulty aroused. My father was too happy at my escape to blame me for the means I resorted to to preserve myself from my hungry foes; and I was forgiven my ill-judged pleasantry to the emperor. The latter expressed regret at my severe punishment for so trifling an offence, but was much amused by my relation of the battle with the rats; he said, he had been startled by observing a huge one jumping out of his hat, as he was in the act of putting it on. On a subsequent occasion, I was confined during the day in the same prison that had been the scene of my nocturnal encounter. Having excited my father's ire for some mischievous trick, and for which, in spite of Napoleon's remonstrances, I was to be condemned to a week's imprisonment, I was taken to my cell every morning, and released at night only to go to bed. The emperor's great amusement during that time was to converse with me through my grated window, and he generally succeeded in making me laugh, by mimicking my dolorous countenance. He was much surprised and amused to find me, on the third day of my imprisonment, busily employed making myself a dress; and was more astonished still when I told him it was a voluntary act; that I had, in a fit of desperation at the dullness of my *séjour* in the cellar, begged my old black nurse, Sarah, to give me some work. I regret that my fit of industry did not survive the term of my incarceration.

The emperor advised my mother to keep the dress I had made during my imprisonment, and occasionally exhibit it to me, when I was contemplating any rash act which might bring down a renewal of my late punishment. He always denominated it the prison livery.

CHAPTER XVIII

Napoleon was a tolerable mimic: one day he asked my sister if she had ever heard the London cries; on her replying she had, he began imitating, them, very much to our diversion. He did it well in all, save the pronunciation of the English, which sounded very droll. My sister said she was sure he must have visited England *incog.* to have acquired them so perfectly. He said he had been much entertained by one of his buffo actors introducing the cries of London, in some comedy which was got up in Paris.

Napoleon was a great admirer of Talma;[71] he said he was the truest actor to nature that ever trod the boards. He was on very intimate and familiar footing with him. I told him I had heard he took lessons from Talma how he was to sit on his throne. He said he had been often asked if such had been the case, and that he one day mentioned the report to the great actor, at the same time remarking to him, "C'est un signe que je m'y tiens bien." He often spoke of Mademoiselle Georges, whom he represented as being very talented, and transcendently beautiful.

One morning, after having been to a ball, and being consequently very tired, I tried in vain, during one of my Longwood promenades, to find where the emperor had hid himself. I was told he was superintending a ditch which was forming for him, that he might have a walk free from molestation. Thither I bent my steps, and discovered Napoleon contemplating the work, with arms folded, and downcast gaze. He said he intended having a private walk, where he could not be overlooked, and for that purpose had directed the ditch to be constructed. It was so laughable an idea, that we could not help smiling at a man's having a *ditch* to promenade in, but so it was; the work was completed soon after, and he had an unobserved walk, which, when made, we were told he never used. I think my memory in this instance has not failed me.

After the earthquake; from sitting on the steps of the veranda, I caught a violent cold, and was sneezing and coughing all the morning. Napoleon said the climate was so bad it was not to be wondered at, and that we ought to have fireplaces made at the Briars, to keep out the cold in the wintry season. I told him it would be useless, as there were no coals on our island. He said we had better then burn some of the orange trees. He was in a bad humour that morning, or he would never have affronted us so much by bidding us destroy our garden, and grub up our beautiful orange trees to burn.

I remember one of Napoleon's favourite contemplations was the history of great men who had figured in bygone days. He told me an anecdote of Cardinal Richelieu, which impressed us much at the time it was repeated to us. It was during the days of his (I may call it) sovereignty, that a nobleman, who waited upon him about affairs of importance, was ushered into his private cabinet. Whilst they were conversing together, a great personage was announced, and entered the room; after some conversation with the cardinal, the great man took his leave, and Richelieu, in compliment to him, attended him to his carriage, forgetting that he had left the other alone in the cabinet. On his return to his room he rang a bell, one of his confidential secretaries entered, to whom he whispered something. He then conversed with the other very freely, appeared to take an interest in his affairs, kept him in conversation for a short time, accompanied him to the door, shook hands with him, and took leave of him in the most friendly way, telling him he might make his mind easy, as he had determined to provide for him. The poor man departed highly satisfied, and full of thanks and gratitude. As he was going out of the door, he was arrested, not allowed to speak to anyone, and conveyed in a coach to the Bastille, where he was kept *au secret* for ten years; at the expiration of which time the cardinal sent for him, and expressed his great regret at having been obliged to adopt the step he had taken; that he had no cause of complaint against him; on the contrary, he believed him to be a good subject to his majesty; but the fact was, he had left a paper on his table when he quitted the room, containing state accounts of vast importance, which he was afraid he might have perused in his absence; that the safety of the kingdom demanded they should not be divulged, and obliged him to adopt measures to prevent the possibility of the contents being known; that as soon as the safety of the country permitted, he had released him; was sorry, and begged his pardon for the uneasiness he had caused him, and would be happy to make him some amends.

The Commissary General of St Helena was a great favourite with everyone who had the pleasure of being acquainted with him.[72] He was most amusing, and very clever. He established a theatre on the island, and the amateur plays performed by him, assisted by the officers of the 53rd and 66th regiments stationed there, rendered the little island a scene of gaiety and continued merriment; what with the races, balls, plays, and picnics, sham fights by sea and land, etc., there was scarcely a day undiversified by some amusement or other. On one memorable occasion, Mr I. invited a large party to picnic at his house; nearly all the inhabitants St Helena contained (who delighted in those pleasurable amusements) were there. The house was situated near the celebrated "Friar's Valley," at a great distance from any of the dwellings of the people bidden to the fête, and the roads leading thereto *must be seen* to be conceived. No language, however romantic in its flight, could impress the reader with the varied dangers and difficulties with which they abounded, and the temptation must indeed have been great to induce a timid horsewoman to encounter them. The ride there, I recollect, was comparatively easy; the party was so delightful, and the weather so charming, that time was beguiled, and the hours unnumbered stole on, till the faint echo of the Ladder Hill gun stole on our startled senses; for it told the guests there assembled, that the ninth hour had struck, and without the countersign none must venture forth, unless they made up their minds to be taken prisoners, and confined for the night in the first guard house they came near. A consultation was held, and the most daring of the party declared the risk of returning home must be run; amongst the boldest of these was my father; and, being under his command, my mother and sister, with myself, and a large proportion of the guests, mounted their horses and set forward. The night was starlight, but the road so bad and unfrequented, that though for a long while the sentries placed about the heights were eluded, our way was lost. I shall never forget the scrambling and tumbling about, the horses' feet tripping under them every moment, over loose stones. At length, my father hailed a light, which appeared at a short distance before us — a most unlucky circumstance. He was answered by a sentry presenting his musket, and demanding "Who goes there?"

"A friend," says my father. "Advance, friend, and give the countersign." But no countersign had we, and to the alarm-house we were all marched, (a guard-room placed between Longwood and the Briars.) We passed a wretched night in the little hole, eaten up by fleas, mosquitoes, and all sorts of horrible things; but the *most* disagreeable was, the quizzing we were obliged to endure from our acquaintance, who had been wise enough to stay at Cruise Plain, instead of being so foolhardy as to venture forth. Napoleon was highly diverted, and rather pleased with the opportunity it gave him for abusing the strict watch which was set to prevent the possibility of his escaping.

CHAPTER XIX

The thoughtlessness of youth, or the consciousness of being a privileged person, prompted me more than once, whilst conversing with Napoleon, to touch upon tender, if not actually forbidden ground, and to question him about some of the many cruel acts assigned to him; *entr' autres*, the butchery of the Turkish prisoners at Jaffa, and the poisoning the sick in hospital at the same place, came one day on the tapis. I remember well his own explanation of the latter report, which though "an old tale and often told," may not prove the less interesting on that account, when recorded, as far as my memory serves me, in the emperor's own words.

"Before leaving Jaffa," said Napoleon, "and when many of the sick had been embarked, I was informed that there were some in hospital wounded beyond recovery, dangerously ill, and unfit to be moved at any risk. I desired my medical men to hold a consultation as to what steps had best be taken with regard to the unfortunate sufferers, and to send in their opinions to me. The result of this consultation was, that seven-eighths of the soldiers were considered past recovery, and that in all probability few would be alive at the expiration of twenty hours. Moreover, some were afflicted with the plague, and to carry those onward would threaten the whole army with infection, and spread death wherever they appeared, without ameliorating their own sufferings or increasing their chance of recovery, which, indeed, in such cases, was hopeless. On the other hand, to leave then behind was abandoning them to the cruelty of the Turks, who always made it a rule to murder their prisoners with protracted torture. In this emergency, I submitted to Desgenettes the propriety of ending the misery of these victims by a dose of opium. I would have desired such a relief for myself under the same circumstances. I considered it would be an act of mercy to anticipate their fate by only a few hours, ensuring them an end free from pain, and oblivious of the horrors which surrounded and threatened them, rather than a death of dreadful torture. My physician did not enter into my views of the case, and disapproved of the proposal, saying, that his profession was to cure, not to kill. Accordingly I left a rear-guard to protect these unhappy men from the advancing enemy, and they remained till nature had paid her last debt and released the expiring soldiers from their agony." Such is the true, and now almost universally acknowledged version of this atrocious story. "Not that I think it would have been a crime," Napoleon observed, "had opium been administered; on the contrary, I think it would have been a virtue. To leave a few miserables, who could not recover, in order that they might be massacred according to the custom of the Turks, with the most dreadful tortures, would I think have been cruelty; nor would any man under similar circumstances, who had the free use of his senses, have hesitated to prefer dying easily a few hours sooner, rather than expire under the tortures of those barbarians. I ask you, O'Meara, to place yourself in the situation of one of these men, and were it demanded of you which fate you would select, either to be left to suffer the tortures of those miscreants, or to have opium administered to you, which would you rather choose? If my own son, and I believe I love my son as well as any father does his child, were in a similar situation, I would advise it to be done; and if so situated myself, I would *insist* upon it, if I had sense enough and strength to demand it. Do you think if I had been capable of secretly poisoning my soldiers, or of such barbarities, (as have been ascribed to me,) of driving my carriage over the mutilated and bleeding bodies of the wounded, — that my troops would have fought under me with the enthusiasm and affection they uniformly displayed? No, no; I should have been shot long ago; even my wounded would have tried to pull a trigger to despatch me."

It is be regretted that the conscience of Napoleon did not prompt him to feel or say with Richard III,

> "E'en all mankind to some lov'd ills incline;
> Great men choose greater things, ambition's mine."

There are many reasons why the worst features of this report were at first readily believed. It was consistent with Napoleon's character to look at results rather than at the measures that were to produce them, and to consider in many cases the end as an excuse for the means; besides, not three months before, he had given the world a fearful example of how bloody a deed he was capable, when he considered it necessary to the furtherance of his own plans. The execution of the Turkish prisoners at Jaffa was equal in cruelty, though not in extent, to the fusillades of the revolution. Besides which, it was unjustifiable by the usages of war, the Turks having given up their arms and surrendered themselves prisoners of war on condition of safety of life at least. It is true that this dreadful deed will always remain a deep stain upon Napoleon's character, but it would be uncharitable to view it as the indulgence of an innate love of cruelty, for nothing in Bonaparte's history shows the existence of such a vice. It was one of the numerous and sad results of boundless ambition, united to unlimited power. In aiming at gigantic undertakings, he forgot to calculate the waste of human life which the execution of his projects necessarily involved.

There was a lady, the wife of an officer in the 66th regiment, a Mrs Baird,[73] who sang and played very well; among her favourite songs was a monody upon the Duke d'Enghien. I learned this, and sang it to Napoleon one day at Madame Bertrand's. He was pleased with the air, and asked me what it was. I showed it to him: there was a vignette on the cover of the music, representing a man standing in a ditch, with a bandage round his eyes and a lantern tied to his waist; in front of him several soldiers, with their muskets levelled in the act of firing. He asked what it meant. I told him it was intended to represent the murder of the Duke d'Enghien. He looked at the print with great interest, and asked me what I knew about it. I told him he was considered the murderer of that illustrious prince. He said, in reply, it was true, he had ordered his execution, for he was a conspirator, and had landed troops in the pay of the Bourbons to assassinate him; and he thought from such a conspiracy, he could not act in a more politic manner than by causing one of their own princes to be put to death, in order the more effectually to deter them from attempting his life again, that the prisoner was tried for having borne arms against the republic, and was executed according to the existing laws; but not, as here represented, in a ditch, and at night. There was nothing secret in the transaction; all was public and open.

I told him I had heard that he wore armour under his dress, to render him invulnerable, as he was continually in dread of assassination, and that he never slept two nights together in the same bedroom. He told us all these things were fabrications; but that he ever adopted one rule — never to make public his intention whither he meant to go, five minutes before he actually took his departure, and he doubted not many conspirators were thus foiled, as they were ignorant where he was at any time to be found.

There was a sculptor named Caracchi, a Corsican, who had once made a statue of him, and who at one time had been strongly attached to Napoleon; but having become a fanatical republican, determined to kill him. For that purpose he went to Paris, and begged to be allowed to model another statue for him, saying, the first was not as well done as he could have desired.

Napoleon, little thinking this man meant to assassinate him, only refused his consent because he did not like the trouble of sitting in the same posture for some days. This saved his life, as it was Caracchi's intention to have poniarded[74] him whilst sitting.

Another time, a letter was sent to inform the emperor that a certain person was to leave at a stated time for Paris, where he would arrive on a day indicated in the letter, his intentions being to murder him. The police took measures, and watched him; he arrived on the day noted, and was seen to enter a chapel whither Napoleon had gone, in celebration of some festival. He was arrested, and expressed his intentions, and said, when the people knelt down on the elevation of the host, he observed the emperor gazing on a beautiful woman. At first, he intended to advance and fire; but, upon reflection, thought it would make it surer to stab him when coming out of chapel. "I forgave the wretch, for I never liked to execute, if I could save life, and merely ordered him to be put in confinement. After leaving France for Elba, I heard he had been ill treated by the other party at the head of affairs, and had escaped. On my return to Paris from Elba, retiring one night to my chamber, the same man somehow or other obtained entrance; by some accident he fell, and the fall caused something in his pocket, which was intended to despatch me, to explode, wounded him so severely instead, that he nearly died. I heard afterwards, that he had thrown himself into the Seine, and was drowned."

CHAPTER XX

In consequence of my mother's health declining, from the enfeebling effects of the too warm climate of St Helena, she was ordered by her medical adviser to try a voyage to England, as the only means of restoring her shattered constitution. The *Winchelsea* store-ship having arrived from China, my father took our passage on board, obtaining first, from Sir Hudson Lowe, six months' leave of absence from his duties as purveyor to Napoleon and his suite, etc.

A day or two before we embarked, my father, my sister, and myself rode to Longwood, to bid adieu to the emperor. He was in his billiard room, surrounded by books, which had arrived a few days before. He seemed much depressed at our leaving the island, and said he sincerely regretted the cause; he hoped my dear mother's health would soon be restored, and sent many affectionate messages to her, she being too ill to accompany us to Longwood. When we had sat with him some time, he walked with us in his garden, and with a sickly smile pointed to the ocean spread out before us, bounding the view, and said, "Soon you will be sailing away towards England, leaving me to die on this miserable rock. Look at those dreadful mountains — they are my prison walls. You will soon hear that the Emperor Napoleon is dead." I burst into tears, and sobbed, as though my heart would break. He seemed much moved at the sorrow manifested by us. I had left my handkerchief in the pocket of my side-saddle, and seeing the tears run fast down my checks, Napoleon took his own from his pocket and wiped them away, telling me to keep the handkerchief in remembrance of that sad day.

We afterwards returned and dined with him. My heart was too full of grief to swallow; and when pressed by Napoleon to eat some of my favourite bon-bons and creams, I told him my throat had a great swelling in it, and I could take nothing.

The hour of bidding adieu came at last. He affectionately embraced my sister and myself, and bade us not forget him; adding that he should ever remember our friendship and kindness to him, and thanked us again and again for all the happy hours he had passed in our society. He asked me what I should like to have in remembrance of him. I replied, I should value a lock of his hair more than any other gift he could present. He then sent for Monsieur Marchand, and desired him to bring in a pair of scissors and cut off four locks of hair for my father and mother, my sister, and myself, which he did. I still possess that lock of hair; it is all left me of the many tokens of remembrance of the Great Emperor.

CHAPTER XXI

In concluding my brief record of Napoleon, I will spare my readers any lengthened expression of my own opinion of his character. I have placed before them the greater part of what occurred while I was in his society, and have thus given them, as far as I am able, the same means of judging of him as I myself possess. But yet, in a personal intercourse, incidents occur, of too trivial or subtle a nature to he communicated to others, but which are still the truest indications of character, from being the result of impulse, and unpremeditated. Even a look, a tone of the voice, a gesture, in an unreserved moment, will give an insight into the real disposition, which years of a more formal intercourse would fail to convey; and this is particularly the case in the association of a person of mature age with very young people. There is generally a confiding candour and openness about them which invites confidence in return, and which tempts a man of the world to throw off the iron mask of reserve and caution, and to assume once more the simplicity of a little child. This, at least, took place in my intercourse with Napoleon, and I may therefore perhaps venture to say a few words on the general impression he left on my mind after three months' daily communication with him.

The point of character which has, more than any other, been a subject of dispute between Napoleon's friends and his enemies, and which will ever be the most important of all, in the estimation of a woman, is, whether he furnished another proof of the "close affinity between superlative intellect and the warmth of the generous affections," (to use the words of the Rev. — Crabbe, in his delightful Life of his Father,) or whether he must be considered only as a consummate calculating machine, the reasoning power perfect, but the heart altogether absent. Bourrienne, who, although conscientious and exact in the main, exhibits no partiality to the emperor, describes him is "trés peu aimant," and reports that he once said, "I have no friend except Duroc, who is unfeeling and cold, and suits me;" and this may have been true in his intercourse with the world, and with men whom he was accustomed to consider as mere machines, the instruments of his glory and ambition, and whom he therefore valued in proportion to the sternness of the stuff of which they were composed. Even his brothers, whom he is said to have included in this sweeping abnegation of friendship, he taught himself to look upon as the means of carrying out his ambitious projects; and as they were not always subservient to his will, but came at times into political collision with him, his fraternal affection, which seldom resisted the rude shocks of contending worldly interests, was cooled and weakened in the struggle. But my own conviction is, that unless Napoleon's ambition, to which every other consideration was sacrificed, interfered, he was possessed of much sensibility and feeling, and was capable of strong attachment.

The Duchess d'Abrantès, who was intimately acquainted with Napoleon at an early age, gives him credit for much more warmth of heart than is allowed to him by the world; and brought up, as she had been, with himself and his family, she was well qualified to form an opinion of him. I think his love of children, and the delight he felt in their society, — and that, too, at the most calamitous period of his life, when a cold and unattachable nature would have been abandoned to the indulgence of selfish misery, in itself, speaks volumes for his goodness of heart. After hours of laborious occupation, he would often permit us to join him, and that which would have fatigued and exhausted the spirits of others, seemed only to recruit and renovate him. His gaiety was often exuberant at these moments; he entered into all the feelings of young people, and when with them was a mere child, and, I may add, a most amusing one.

I feel, however, even painfully, the difficulty of conveying to my readers my own impression of the disposition of Napoleon. Matters of feeling are often incapable of demonstration. The innumerable acts of amiability and kindness which he lavished on all around him at my father's house, derived, perhaps, their chief charm from the way in which they were done; they would not bear being told. Apart from the sweetness of his smile and manner, their effect would have been comparatively nothing. But young people are generally keen observers of character. Their perceptive faculties are ever on the alert, and their powers of observation not the less acute, perhaps, because their reason lies dormant, and there is nothing to interrupt the exercise of their perceptions. And after seeing Napoleon in every possible mood, and in his most unguarded moments, when I am sure, from his manner, that the idea of acting a part never entered his head, I left, him, impressed with the most complete conviction of his want of guile, and the thorough amiability and goodness of his heart. That this feeling was common to almost everyone who approached him, the respect and devotion of his followers at St Helena is a sufficient proof. They had then nothing more to expect from him, and only entailed misery on themselves by adhering to his fortunes.

Shortly after he left the Briars for Longwood, I was witness to an instance of the reverence with which he was regarded by those around him. A lady of high distinction at St Helena,[75] whose husband filled one of the diplomatic offices there, rode up one morning to the Briars. I happened to be on the lawn, and she requested me to show her the part of the cottage occupied by the emperor. I conducted her to the pavilion, which she surveyed with intense interest; but when I pointed out to her the crown which bad been cut from the turf by his faithful adherents, she lost all control over her, feelings. Bursting into a fit of passionate weeping, she sank on her knees upon the ground, sobbing hysterically. At last she fell forward, and I became quite alarmed, and would have run to the cottage to tell my mother and procure some restoratives, but, starting up, she implored me, in a voice broken by emotion, to call no one, for that she should soon be herself again. She entreated me not to mention to anyone what had occurred, and proceeded to say that the memory of Napoleon was treasured in the hearts of the French people as it was in hers, and that they would all willingly die for him. She was herself a Frenchwoman, and very beautiful. She recovered herself after some time, and put a thousand questions to me about Napoleon, the answers to which seemed to interest her exceedingly. She said several times, "How happy it must have made you to be with the emperor!" After a long interview, she put a thick veil down over her still agitated features, and returning to her horse, mounted and rode away. For once, I kept a secret, and, though questioned on the subject, I merely said she had come to see the pavilion, without betraying what had taken place.

Napoleon, on his first arrival, showed an inclination to mix in what little society St Helena afforded, and would, I think, have continued to do so, but for the unhappy differences with Sir Hudson Lowe. These at length grew to such a height, that the emperor seemed to consider it almost a point of honour to shut himself up, and make himself as miserable as possible, in order to excite indignation against the governor. Into the merits of these quarrels, it is not my intention to enter. With all my feeling of partiality for the emperor, I have often doubted whether any human being could have filled the situation of Sir Hudson Lowe without becoming embroiled with his unhappy captive. The very title by which he was accosted, and the manner of addressing him, when contrasted with the devotion. of those around him, must have seemed almost insulting; and the emperor was most *brusque* and uncompromising in showing his dislike to anyone who did not please him; the necessary restrictions on his personal liberty would always have been a fruitful source of discord; and even had Napoleon himself been inclined to submit to his fate with equanimity, it is doubtful whether his followers would have permitted him to do so. Accustomed as they had been to the gaiety and brilliancy of the French capital, their "séjour," to use their own words, on that lone island, could not fail to he "affreux"; and as they were generally the medium of communication between Napoleon and the authorities, the correspondence would necessarily be tinged with more or less of the bitterness of their respective feelings. Their very devotion to the emperor would make them too tenacious and exacting with regard to the deference to which his situation entitled him; and thus orders and regulations, which only seemed to the authorities indispensable to his security, became a crime in their eyes, and were represented to the emperor as gratuitous and cruel insults. Napoleon, too, in the absence of everything more worthy of supplying food to his mighty intellect, did not disdain to interest himself in the merest trifles. My father has often described him as appearing as much absorbed and occupied in the details of some petty squabble with the governor as if the fate of empires had been under discussion. He has often made us laugh with his account of the ridiculous way in which Napoleon spoke of Sir Hudson Lowe; but their disputes were generally on subjects so trivial, that I deem it my duty to draw a veil over these last infirmities of so noble a mind.

One circumstance, however, I may relate: Napoleon, wishing to learn English, procured some English books; amongst them "Æsop's Fables," were sent him. In one of the fables the sick lion, after submitting with fortitude to the insults of the many animals who came to exult over his fallen greatness, at last received a kick in the face from the ass. "I could have borne everything but this," the lion said. Napoleon showed the wood-cut, and added, "It is me and your governor."

Amongst other accusations against Napoleon, some writers have said that he was deficient in courage. He always gave me the idea, on the contrary, of being constitutionally fearless. I have already mentioned his feats of horsemanship, and the speed with which his carriage generally tore along the narrow mountainous roads of St Helena would have been intolerable to a timid person. I have more than once seen gentlemen, whose horses were rather skittish, when the emperor approached them at a rapid pace, compelled to turn and gallop rapidly for some distance before him, to their great annoyance, until they reached an open space where they could pass his carriage without danger of their horses shying and going down a precipice.

He had a description of jaunting-car, to which he yoked three Cape horses abreast, in the French style, and if he got anyone into this, he seldom let his victim out until he had frightened him heartily. One day he told General Gourgaud to make his horse rear and put his fore feet into the carriage, to my great terror. He seemed, indeed, to possess no nerves himself, and to laugh at the existence of fear in others.

Napoleon, as far as I was capable of judging, could not be considered fond of literature. He seldom introduced the topic in conversation, and I suspect his reading was confined almost solely to scientific subjects. I have heard him speak slightingly of poets, and call them *réveurs*, and still I believe the most visionary of them all, was the only one he ever perused. But his own vast and undefined schemes of ambition, seemed to have found something congenial in the dreamy sublimities of Ossian.

THE END

END NOTES

1. The *Icarus* was a 90 foot brig-sloop of ten guns. It was built in 1814 and the senior officer was Commander Thomas Barker Devon. *Icarus* saw service at St Helena and then went on to the East Indies. It was sold out of Royal Navy service in 1838. Thomas Barker Devon, (1784-1846) entered the Royal Navy in 1797, rising to captain in 1825.

2. Sir George Cockburn, eighth baronet, (1772-1853). Cockburn joined the Royal Navy in 1786 and by 1814 had risen to the rank of Rear Admiral. In August 1814, Cockburn accompanied the joint naval and military force under Major-General Ross, which after the battle of Bladensburg seized the city of Washington for twenty-four hours. Cockburn also accompanied Ross in the subsequent advance against Baltimore, and was with him in the skirmish on 12 September in which Ross was mortally wounded. Between January and March 1815, while Cochrane attempted to take New Orleans, Cockburn undertook diversionary attacks on the coast of Georgia from a base on Cumberland Island. He was recalled to England following the conclusion of peace, only to find, on anchoring at Spithead on 4 May, that war with France had again broken out. He was ordered to hoist his flag on board HMS *Northumberland* and to convey Napoleon to St Helena, which he reached on 15 October. He remained there as governor of the island and commander-in-chief of the Cape of Good Hope station until the summer of 1816, when he was relieved by Sir Hudson Lowe and Sir Pulteney Malcolm. He was a junior lord of the Admiralty between April 1818 and May 1827, a member of the council of the lord high admiral between May 1827 and September 1828, and then first naval lord until November 1830.

3. HMS *Havannah* was a Royal Navy 36-gun fifth-rate frigate. She was launched at the Liverpool yard of Wilson & Co. in 1811 and was one of twenty-seven Apollo-class frigates. She was cut down to a 24-gun sixth rate in 1845, converted to a training ship in 1860 and sold for breaking in 1905. On 19 July 1815, *Havannah* was in company with *Sealark, Rhin, Menelaus, Fly* and *Ferret* when they captured the French vessels *Fortune, Papillon, Marie Graty, Marie Victorine, Cannoniere,* and *Printemis*. It is unclear precisely who this Captain Hamilton was.

4. Surtout — a man's outer coat.

5. Henri-Gatien, Comte Bertrand, (1773-1844). Henri-Gatien Bertrand was born at Châteauroux, a member of a well-to-do bourgeois family. At the outbreak of the French Revolution, he had just finished his studies at the Prytanée National Militaire, and he entered the army as a volunteer. During the expedition to

Egypt, Napoleon named him colonel (1798), then brigadier-general, and after the Battle of Austerlitz his aide-de-camp. His life was henceforth closely bound up with that of Napoleon, who had the fullest confidence in him, honouring him in 1808 with the title of count and at the end of 1813, with the title of Grand Marshal of the Palace. It was Bertrand who in 1809 directed the building of the bridges by which the French army crossed the Danube at Wagram. In 1811, Bertrand was appointed governor for Illyria and during the German campaign of 1813, he commanded IV Corps which he led in the battles of Grossbeeren, Dennewitz and Leipzig. In 1813, after the Battle of Leipzig, it was due to his initiative that the French army was not totally destroyed. He accompanied Napoleon to Elba in 1814, returned with him in 1815, held a command in the Waterloo campaign, and then, after the defeat, accompanied Napoleon to St Helena. Condemned to death in 1816, he did not return to France until after Napoleon's death, and then Louis XVIII granted him amnesty allowing him to retain his rank. Bertrand was elected deputy in 1830 but defeated in 1834. In 1840 he was chosen to accompany the prince de Joinville to St Helena to retrieve and bring Napoleon's remains to France, in what became known as the retour des cendres.

The Bertrand children provided the most constant enjoyment for Napoleon. General Henri Gatien Bertrand, known in Napoleon's Imperial household as "The Grand Marshal", married Fanny Bertrand in 1808. They arrived with three children and settled in a small villa called Hutt's Gate, a mile away from Longwood. A fourth child, Arthur, was born on St Helena in 1817. The Bertrands, particularly the countess, were hoping to limit their stay on the island to not more than a year because of the education needs of their children: Henri aged three, Hortense aged five, and Napoleon aged seven. They had agreed to follow the Emperor into exile before the final destination had been announced, hoping, as did Napoleon, that the final destination would be England. Nevertheless, the Bertrands, who had also accompanied Napoleon to Elba, would stay with Napoleon to the very end. Fanny gave birth to their fourth child Arthur in 1817, and he became Napoleon's favourite member of the family.

6. Gaspard Gourgaud, (1783-1852). Gaspard, Baron Gourgaud, was born at Versailles; his father was a musician of the royal chapel. At school he showed talent in mathematical studies and later joined the artillery. In 1802 he became junior lieutenant, and thereafter served with credit in the campaigns of 1803-1805, being wounded at Austerlitz. He was present at the siege of Saragossa in 1808, returned to service in Central Europe. In 1811 he became one of the ordnance officers attached to Napoleon, whom he followed closely through the Russian campaign of 1812; he was one of the first to enter the Kremlin. For his services in this campaign he received the title of baron, and became first ordnance officer. In the campaign of 1813 in Saxony he again showed courage and prowess, especially at Leipzig and Hanau; but it was in the first battle of 1814, near to Brienne, that he rendered the most signal service by killing the leader of a small band of Cossacks who were riding furiously towards Napoleon's tent.

Wounded at the Battle of Montmirail, he recovered in time to be involved in several of the conflicts which followed, distinguishing himself especially at Laon and Reims. Though enrolled among the royal guards of King Louis XVIII of France in the summer of 1814, he embraced the cause of Napoleon during the Hundred Days, was named general and aide-de-camp by Napoleon, and fought at Waterloo.

After the second abdication of the emperor in June 1815, Gourgaud retired with him to Rochefort. It was to Gourgaud that Napoleon entrusted the letter of appeal to the Prince Regent for asylum in England. Gourgaud set off in HMS *Slaney*, but was not allowed to land in England. Determined to share Napoleon's exile, he sailed with him on HMS *Northumberland* to Saint Helena.

7. Emmanuel-Augustin-Dieudonné-Joseph, (1766-1842). He was born into a noble family at the castle of Las Cases in Languedoc and educated at the military schools of Vendôme and Paris. After entering the French Royal Navy he took part in various engagements during 1781-1782. Following the outbreak of the Revolution he emigrated, and he spent some years in Germany and ended up in England.

    In 1801 he published in English the original edition of his famous atlas, but following the Peace of Amiens he returned to Paris and issued the first French edition in 1803-1804, called *Atlas historique, genealogique, chronologique et geographique*. The atlas made Las Cases rich. It came to Napoleon's notice only when, in Las Cases's company, he went into exile on St. Helena.

    Not until 1810 did he receive much notice from Napoleon's government, which then made him a chamberlain and created him a count of the empire. After the first abdication of the emperor Las Cases retired to England, but returned to serve Napoleon during the Hundred Days. Following the second abdication he withdrew with Napoleon and a few other trusty followers to Rochefort, and then onwards to St Helena. He brought along his eldest son, 14-year-old Emmanuel, "with an intelligence far above his years," according to one historian. Las Cases spoke English — an important asset to Bonaparte. Usually referred to as "young Las Cases," the boy assisted his father in taking down Napoleon's memoirs which thereafter took form in the famous *Mémorial de Ste Hélène*.

    Las Cases left St Helena in 1816, and after a short spell at Cape Town he returned to Europe and lived at first at Brussels and later at Paris where he published the *Mémorial*, and soon gained great wealth from it. In 1840 when the expedition set sail for St Helena to bring back Napoleon's body, he was too ill to go, but young Emmanuel who had shared his captivity was able to go.

8. Napoléon François Joseph Charles Bonaparte, (1811-1832). Napoleon II was born at the Tuileries Palace in Paris to Emperor Napoleon and his second wife, Marie Louise of Austria. As Napoleon I's eldest legitimate son, he was already constitutionally Prince Imperial and heir-apparent, but the Emperor also gave his son the style "His Majesty the King of Rome". Three years later, the First French Empire, to which he was heir, collapsed. Napoleon abdicated the throne in favour of his toddler son, but the Allied Powers, at the insistence of Emperor

Alexander I of Russia, refused to recognise the three-year-old as monarch. In April 1814 Marie Louise retired to Austria with young Napoleon. He died of tuberculosis at Schönbrunn Palace in Vienna in 1832. The Emperor Napoleon never saw his son again after 1814.

9. Charles Robert George Hodson, (1779-1858). Hodson was a major of the St. Helena Regiment, and Judge Advocate. He was in St. Helena during the whole of the captivity, and before that time he had filled the position of Town Major. He was a tall man, over six feet in height, and of imposing appearance. For these reasons Napoleon, who had for him a warm personal regard, styled him "Hercules." On 20 November 1815, the evening of Sir George Cockburn's ball, Napoleon paid him a visit at his house, and on 4 January 1816, he entertained him and his wife at dinner at Longwood. Hodson was present at the funeral of Napoleon, and also at the exhumation in 1840.

10. *Marchandes de modes* — a term only very inadequately translated as "milliner".

11. Dominique Jean Larrey, (1766-1842). Larrey was surgeon-in-chief of the Napoleonic armies from Italy in 1797 to Waterloo in 1815. During this time, he initiated the modern method of army surgery, field hospitals and the system of army ambulance corps. After seeing the speed with which the carriages of the French flying artillery manoeuvred across the battlefields, Larrey adapted them as Flying Ambulances for rapid transport of the wounded and manned them with trained crews of drivers, corpsmen and litter-bearers. He established a rule for war casualties, treating the wounded according to the seriousness of their injuries and urgency of need for medical care, regardless of their rank or nationality. Soldiers of enemy armies, as well as those of the French and their allies, were treated. He was made a Commandeur of the Légion d'honneur in 1807. At Waterloo in 1815 his courage under fire was noticed by the Duke of Wellington who ordered his soldiers not to fire in his direction so as to "give the brave man time to gather up the wounded".

12. Thomas William Poppleton, (1775-1827). Poppleton, was the orderly officer of Longwood, who received the "Emperor's Snuff Box" from Napoleon. Poppleton, born in England in 1775, served with general Daumier's regiment, while stationed in Galway. He married, Margaret, daughter of Nicholas Martin of Ross. Subsequently he transferred to the 53rd Foot Regiment, and served in Egypt, and took part in Baird's famous Desert March to India. Having served in the Peninsular Wars, he was appointed orderly officer at Longwood in St Helena and served in this capacity from 10 December 1815 to 24 July 1817. The 53rd (Shropshire) Regiment, or a battalion thereof, was later sent to St Helena to guard Napoleon, who called the Regiment the "Red Regiment", a reference to the colour of their facings, which also gave rise to the Regiment's nickname, the "Brickdusts". One anecdote relates Napoleon's attempt to escape, but the fact is that Napoleon was merely playing with his captor. Napoleon being an expert cavalry rider, and Captain Poppleton (the Captain on guard) only an infantry officer, and little accustomed to riding manoeuvres, the latter had been left far behind by his companion in one of the airings. Napoleon

it seems enjoyed most heartily the triumph of galloping away from his keeper, who could only bear the simple jog-trot of his Rosinante. Napoleon had really exceeded the length of his chain, made some romantic and chivalric leaps in his progress, and had climbed some dreadful steeps. Poppleton is said to have been incensed at his conduct, and made a report to the Admiral. The unlucky evil-doer was not allowed to ride out with the Captain for some time, and he was assured, by a rough message from the Admiral, that if he transgressed in such a way again, the sentinels had orders to level him to the earth. It seems that despite this, the two men became friends and Napoleon made a gift of his snuff box to Poppleton.

13. Charles Tristan, marquis de Montholon, (1782-1853). Entering the army in 1797, Montholon rose with rapidity and avowed himself, when chef d'escadron in Paris at the time of the coup d'état of November 1799, entirely devoted to Napoleon. He served at the Battle of Jena and distinguishing himself at the battle of Aspern-Essling where he was wounded. At the end of that campaign on the Danube he received the title of count and remained in close attendance on Napoleon, who confided to him several important duties. He was chosen for a mission to discuss diplomatic matters with the Austrian commander Archduke Ferdinand Karl Joseph of Austria-Este at Würzburg among others. At the time of the first abdication of Napoleon at Fontainebleau, Montholon was one of the few generals who advocated one more attempt to rally the French troops for the overthrow of the allies. In exile with Napoleon after the second abdication he, with his wife, Albine de Montholon, accompanied the emperor to Rochefort, where Napoleon and his friends finally adopted the proposal, which emanated from Count Las Cases, that he should throw himself on the generosity of the British nation and surrender to HMS *Bellerophon*. Montholon and his wife accompanied the ex-emperor to St Helena. Napoleon chiefly dictated to Montholon the notes on his career which form so interesting, though far from trustworthy, a commentary on the events of the first part of his life. Montholon is known to have despised and flouted Las Cases, though in later writings he affected to laud his services to Napoleon. With Gourgaud, who was no less vain and sensitive than himself, there was a standing feud which would have led to a duel but for the express prohibition of Napoleon. Las Cases left the island in November 1816, and Gourgaud in January 1818; but Montholon, despite the departure of his wife, stayed on at Longwood to the end of the emperor's life. Those who believe that Napoleon was murdered by poisoning now regard Montholon — despite his assumed devotion to Napoleon — as the most likely suspect.

14. Achille Thomas L'Union Archambault, (1794-1858) and his younger brother Joseph Olivier Archambault, (1796-1874) both accompanied Napoleon to St Helena working in the stables under the command of General Gourgaud. The younger brother spent only a short time in the service of Napoleon, but under his instructions followed Joseph Bonaparte to America, where he settled, prospered, and raised a family. Achille was among the party who returned to St Helena in 1840 to bring home Napoleon's remains.

15. Leporello — a character from *Don Giovanni*, an opera with music by Wolfgang Amadeus Mozart and with an Italian libretto by Lorenzo Da Ponte.

16. Scaramouche — a roguish clown character of the Italian commedia dell'arte who wears a black mask and black trousers, shirt and hat. The character was invented by a seventeenth-century Italian actor, Tiberio Fiorelli.

17. Napoleon aged seven, Hortense aged five, and Henri aged three.

18. Jean Baptiste Cipriani, also called Cipriani Franceschi or Franceschi Cipriani, (d. 1818), was Corsican and rumoured to be Napoleon's half-brother. According to author Norwood Young (1915) Cipriani Franceschi, known as Cipriani, was a Corsican, who had been a secret agent, or spy, in Capri and neighbourhood during the time that Sir Hudson Lowe was Governor of the island; he claimed to have outwitted the Englishman. He went to Elba with Napoleon as a valet. He was now the major-domo. Though without education, he was a man of some natural ability. Napoleon had great confidence in him, and he was closely attached to the Bonapartes; his son was in attendance on Cardinal Fesch at Rome, and his daughter with Madame Letizia, Madame Mère.

    On 24 February 1818, Cipriani fell ill without warning, though he was always in perfect health. He was seized with violent pains in the stomach and with very cold chills. They placed him in hot baths. Chills and stomach pains are signs of acute arsenical intoxication. Two days later, at 4:00 p.m., he died. Cipriani was buried immediately, but somebody must have exhumed his body, for it is rumoured to have disappeared. Among conspiracy theories, it is assumed that somebody was concerned that a post mortem would show up poisoning, because it is easy to detect acute arsenical intoxication. According to the late Dr Ben Weider, his death proves that there was a poisoner on the island living at Longwood House. Dr Weider also suggests that Cipriani was really Napoleon's secret agent. Authors Thierry Lentz and Peter Hicks have also contributed an interesting article on the subject.

    On the night of 14 October 1840, on St Helena, in the driving rain, Napoleon's tomb was opened and one of history's greatest mysteries was awakened. How did Napoleon, the man of war and pioneering military strategy, die? Was he poisoned and if so, by whom? Why were there so many discrepancies between the official records of his burial and exhumation? And why does Napoleon's death mask bear a greater resemblance to his childhood friend, Cipriani, rumoured to be his half brother, than to any of Napoleon's portraits? In 2002, Bruno Rey-Henri, a lawyer and historian, asked for the corpse to be dug up after concluding in a book that DNA testing was the only way to resolve the heated 30-year debate, but permission was refused. He and others say there are too many inconsistencies surrounding Napoleon's burial on St Helena in 1821 and the body's exhumation and transfer to Paris in 1840. He says Napoleon's real remains were probably taken to Westminster Abbey by his British captors, and the body buried in Paris was actually that of his maitre-d'hotel, Jean-Baptiste Cipriani.

19. Jean Abram Noverraz, (1790-1849). Novveraz was third valet at Longwood. He was a Swiss, and married in July, 1819, Josephine Brule, the femme de

chambre of the Countess de Montholon. He was at Longwood throughout the captivity, and returned for the exhumation.

20. Louis-Joseph Marchand, (1791-1876). Marchand entered service in the Imperial Household in 1811 as garçon d'appartement, subsequently becoming Premier valet de chambre. He followed Napoleon to Elba and then St Helena, becoming one of the key figures in creation of the legend around the fallen emperor. Marchand returned to France in 1821, living out his life easily between Paris and Auxerre. He died in 1876 aged 85.

21. *Causerie* — An informal discussion or chat, especially of an intellectual nature.

22. This reference is to Laura Wilks. The Governor was Colonel Mark Wilks FRS, (1759-1831). Mark Wilks arrived in India on a military commission when he was eighteen and was appointed to the Madras Army. On 20 November 1812 he was appointed governor of St Helena (then still under the East India Company), and he arrived there on 22 June 1813. His administration was firm and enlightened, and he was popular. He improved agriculture by introducing better methods of cultivation, and by persuading the East India Company to alter the land tenure system. He was promoted brevet colonel on 4 June 1814. He was described as, in 1815, "a tall, handsome, venerable-looking man, with white curling locks and a courtier-like manner". He was governor on the arrival of Napoleon on 15 October 1815, but was not made responsible for Napoleon, who continued in the custody of the naval officer who brought him. However, they met and conversed through an interpreter, largely on chemistry and on India. Despite a form of friendship, Wilks refused to take an appeal from Napoleon to the Prince Regent. In April 1816 Wilks was replaced by Sir Hudson Lowe. The Duke of Wellington and others believed that if Wilks had been retained his relations with Napoleon would have been better than Lowe's. He returned to England and retired from the company's service on 15 October 1818. Wilks married twice. His second wife, whom he married at Bath on 16 February 1813, was Miss Dorothy Taubman. With his first wife he had a daughter, Laura (1796/7-1888). She was famous for her beauty, on which she was complimented by Napoleon, who gave her a bracelet.

23. Jean-Dominique Vivant-Denon, (1747-1825). Minister of Arts under Napoleon, developer and first director of the Louvre Museum; collector and engraver.

24. *Parure* — adornment, from parer, to adorn.

25. Count Charles Frederic Jules Piontkowski, (1786-1849). Count Piontkowski arrived at St Helena 29 December 1815 and left on 19 October 1816. Lord Rosebery in his work, whilst outlining some basic facts, dismisses him with, "Piontkowski remains a figure of mystery. He was a trooper in the Polish Lancers, who had followed Napoleon to Elba, and had been given a commission in consequence of his fidelity. At a time when the British Government would not allow Gourgaud to take with him his old servant, or Las Cases to be rejoined by his wife, they sent Piontkowski unbidden and unwelcome to join the Emperor... He vanished as suddenly as he came, nine months afterwards, with, apparently, plenty of money." Telling us that "Napoleon openly suspected him of being a

spy," Rosebery rejects this; adds "but his appearance and career at Longwood still require elucidation." Frédéric Masson summarised Piontkowski this way: "It is difficult to deal with the mysterious Polish officer Piontkowski who, after accompanying the Emperor from Malmaison to Rochefort, followed him to England and then when all his companions — those not allowed to proceed to St Helena — were deported to Malta, succeeded, it is not known under whose patronage or by what influence, in joining Napoleon, found himself suspected at the same time by the English and the French, and after a stay of some months during which time he remained a riddle, was taken back to England: then, as a reward for his six months' hypothetical devotion, received annuities and assistance by means of which he lived in luxury during nearly fifty years of journeying round Europe. At St Helena no one asked for him, no one enquired about him, no one grieved for him and he was verily a mystery-man for whom, for no conceivable reason, obstacles were removed and orders countermanded. He appeared before the Emperor in a uniform to which he had no right, took firm root, and was tolerated. He was a glib liar, quite useless, and he departed with no better reason than he had for coming. He was probably only a sharper — this individual who pulled the legs of the English Government, Emperor Napoleon, Sardinia, Austria, Russia, and the rest of Europe."

26. *Tirailleur* — formerly, a member of an independent body of marksmen in the French army. They were used sometimes in front of the army to annoy the enemy.

27. Sir Hudson Lowe, (1769-1844). Lowe had a long army career which coincidentally included time in Napoleon's native Corsica, where he had been present at the capture in 1794. He remained two years in garrison at Ajaccio, then went with the 50th to Elba, where he was deputy judge-advocate. Subsequently he was stationed in Portugal for two years and became proficient in Portuguese, having already obtained a good knowledge of Spanish. From Lisbon he moved in 1799 to Minorca, where he was made one of the inspectors of foreign corps and put at the head of 200 anti-republican Corsicans — styled the Corsican rangers — with the rank of major-commandant from 5 July 1800. His career continued throughout the wars and in fact he met Napoleon in 1813 when on an inspection of the Russian German Legion — a force composed of German fugitives from the Moscow retreat — which was to be paid by Britain. He remained with the Russian army for the ensuing campaign, being present at the battles of Bautzen where he saw Napoleon. On 24 January 1814 he rejoined Blücher at Vaucouleurs, being subsequently present with the Prussians at thirteen general engagements. As the only British officer of rank with Blücher's army, Lowe was privy to many important deliberations, especially during the conferences at Châtillon, where he strongly advocated the advance on Paris. He was the first officer to bring to England the news of Napoleon's abdication, arriving in London on 9 April 1814, after having ridden from Paris to Calais through potentially hostile country attended by a single cossack. Lowe was knighted on 26 April 1814 and promoted major-general on 4 June.

At Marseilles, on 1 August 1815, Lowe received intimation that he would have the custody of Napoleon, who had taken refuge on the *Bellerophon*, in

Aix Roads, a fortnight previously. On Lowe's departure from Marseilles, the citizens of the town presented him with a silver urn bearing an inscription alluding to his having saved the city from being pillaged. The island of St Helena in the south Atlantic was a possession of the East India Company, and on 23 August the court of directors notified him that they had appointed him governor with a salary of £12,000 a year.

In mid-January 1816 Lowe left Portsmouth for St Helena, accompanied by his wife and her two daughters; they reached the island on 14 April. Two days earlier, a warrant had been issued, addressed to Lowe as "lieutenant-general of his Majesty's army in St Helena and governor of that island", requiring him to detain and keep Napoleon as a prisoner of war, under such directions as should be issued from time to time by one of the principal secretaries of state. Indeed, frequent dispatches from Bathurst would reiterate Napoleon's status as a prisoner and the government's persistent fear that he might again escape captivity, as he had from Elba. Lowe, therefore, felt compelled to restrict Napoleon's freedom of movement. Nevertheless, he was not inhumane: shortly after his arrival, he raised the annual allowance for running Longwood, where Napoleon and his entourage lived, from £8,000 to £12,000. Lowe was unable to establish a satisfactory relationship with Napoleon and his dislike intensified, as Lowe insisted on still-tighter security. Lowe and Napoleon met six times in four months, then no more. The last two encounters were particularly acrimonious; though, by all accounts, Lowe maintained self-control in the face of considerable verbal abuse. After 18 August 1816 he refused to make further visits to Longwood, though a contrary version holds that Napoleon declined to see Lowe again because "he makes me too angry and I lose my dignity". Napoleon also told a nephew of the prime minister, Lord Liverpool, that Lowe "was one of the few men that your uncle should never have sent here", due to his association with "the Corsican battalion", which Napoleon considered a collection of renegades and deserters. Indeed, views similar to Napoleon's were independently expressed. Wellington thought Lowe "a very bad choice ... wanting in education and judgement ... a stupid man ... [who] was suspicious and jealous".

28. Tristan Montholon was just three years old. The duties of running the imperial household fell to General Charles Tristan Montholon, a 32-year-old who had married Albine Helene de Vassal, previously Madame Roger, in 1812. They arrived at St Helena with Tristan, but left behind their baby born the previous year considered too young for the journey and Albine's 12-year-old boy from a previous marriage. She gave birth to a daughter, Napoleone Marie Helene, in 1816. Two years later upon the arrival of Napoleone-Josephine Montholon, there was speculation that the father was Napoleon himself. The Montholon family occupied three rooms at Longwood. Commenting on the household collection, historian John Holland Rose described Tristan as "the bright little boy of the Montholons." According to Alan Schom, Monotholon's presence on the island "was to prove the most disastrous personnel decision of Napoleon's entire life," due to mounting evidence — such as the detective work by Weider,

Forshufvud and Hapgood — pointing toward Monotholon as the one who murdered Napoleon with poison.

29. Nankeen, also called Nankeen cloth, is a kind of pale yellowish cloth, originally made at Nanjing from a yellow variety of cotton, but subsequently manufactured from ordinary cotton which is then dyed. Also in the plural a piece or variety of this cloth. It was later considered a possibility that this cloth gave off arsenic. The wallpaper (or wall covering) used in Longwood contained a high level of arsenic compound used for colouring by British manufacturers. The adhesive, which in the cooler British environment was innocuous, may have grown mould in the more humid climate and emitted the poisonous gas arsine. This theory has been ruled out as it does not explain the arsenic absorption patterns found in other analyses.

30. Napoleone Marie Helene, born in 1816.

31. *Gaucherie* — an awkward or tactless act.

32. *Sottises* — a message that seems to convey no meaning.

33. *Folle* — mad; insane.

34. Brilliants — in this sense small diamonds; the French 'brilliant' was formed of two truncated pyramids placed base to base. This was obviously a valuable gift.

35. Captain Jean Claude de Gor, the A.D.C. to the Marquis de Montchenu, French Commissioner. He arrived with his master in the *Newcastle* on 17 June 1816, and left St Helena 29 July 1821, in the *Lady Melville*.

36. Sir William Webber Doveton, (1753-1843). Member of the Council of St Helena. Doveton was a native of St Helena, and lived at Mount Pleasant, Sandy Bay. He left St Helena for England on 14 March 1818, in the *Marquis of Camden*, and returned on 4 May 1819, in the *Bombay*. During this visit he received a knighthood on account of his public-spirited exertions in connection with the government of the Island, and the East India Company, after debating a whole day, granted him a pension of £800 per annum. Napoleon paid a visit to Sandy Bay on 3 January 1816 and on 4 October 1820 he paid another visit, and had breakfast on the lawn with the Doveton family. This proved to be the last excursion made by Napoleon outside the "limits". Doveton was present at both the funeral in 1821 and the exhumation in 1840.

37. Admiral Henry John Rous, (1795-1877). Rous was educated at Westminster School, and entered the Royal Navy in 1808. Rous came out to St Helena in HMS *Conqueror*, and served in that ship until August 1817, when he was appointed to HMS *Podargus*. He retained this command until January 1818, but was then transferred to HMS *Mosquito*, and in July, 1819, he left St. Helena. Rous, who in later-life became such a power on the Turf, had much to do with the institution of the Races at Deadwood.

During his subsequent naval career he was appointed first to the HMS *Bacchante*. In 1823 he was made captain, and in 1825 given command of HMS *Rainbow*. He served in the Indian and New Holland stations from 1823 to 1829. In April 1827, he organised Sydney's first regatta. In 1834 he was appointed to the command of the HMS *Pique*, a 36-gun frigate, which ran ashore on the coast of Labrador and was greatly damaged. Rous, however, brought her across the Atlantic Ocean with a sprung foremast and without keel, forefoot or rudder. Rous, always fond of the sport became a steward of the Jockey Club in 1838, a position he held almost uninterruptedly to his death. At the 1841 general election, he was elected as MP for Westminster.

38. Laure Junot, Duchess of Abrantès (née Martin de Permond, (1784-1838). Laure Junot was the wife of French general Jean-Andoche Junot. She was the daughter of Charles Martin de Permond and his wife Panoria, to whom during her widowhood the young Napoleon made an offer of marriage. Napoleon visited their house a good deal after the downfall of the Jacobin party in Thermidor 1794.

39. Charles Bayne Hodgson Ross, (1776-1849). Charles Ross joined the Royal Navy in 1788 and served throughout the Napoleonic Wars. Promoted to Captain in 1802, he was given command of HMS *Pique* and captured the French brigs *Phaeton* and *Voltageur* in March 1806. He served in operations in North America in 1814 and later commanded HMS *Northumberland* as she transported Napoleon to exile on St Helena in 1815. He served as Commissioner of Plymouth Dockyard in 1829 and was appointed Commander-in-Chief, Pacific Station in 1837. As Captain of the *Northumberland*, he left St Helena on 19 June 1816.

40. The game of Puss in the Corner requires a room or court, or other square area with four corners, posts, or trees equidistant from one another. One player begins as "Puss" and takes his or her place in the centre of the area. Each of the other four players selects one of the corners and takes his or her place there. Play begins with the four corner players attempting to exchange places with each other in any direction. "Puss" attempts to gain a corner during the exchange. Should "Puss" succeed, the player then left without a corner becomes the new "Puss" and play continues.

41. Josephine Brule, maid to Madame Montholon, and who married Noverraz.

42. Leno — a kind of cotton gauze.

43. Several cooks came to work at Longwood in turn; the first was Michel Lepage, as he came to St Helena with Napoleon in replacement of the normal cook of the imperial service. Lepage was not a good cook; he was later assisted by a Belgian cook woman nicknamed "Jeanette". She was previously employed at Plantation House, the Governor's house; she married Lepage and both left Longwood on 8 June 1818. Then, for some time, Napoleon and his suite had to get used to Chinese food, as there was no other cook speaking French in the island except for La Roche, who remained in the island for some weeks, but left in March 1819. In September 1819, Chandelier, an excellent cook was sent from Rome by Napoleon's sister, Pauline, and started in Napoleon's service; but he had to leave the island a few months later, for health reasons; Longwood then returned to Chinese food!

44. Baron de Barthelemy Sturmer, (1787-1853), the Austrian Commissioner in St Helena. He arrived in the *Orontes* on 18 June 1816, with his wife, née Emmance de Boutet and four servants. They lived at Rosemary Hall — Formerly the residence of Mr W. Wrangham. After other diplomatic posts Sturmer became

Austrian ambassador to Constantinople (1832-1850). He received the title of count in 1842.

45. William Pitt, 1st Earl Amherst, (1775-1857). Lord Amherst sailed in February, 1816, on a special Mission to China, and arrived in Canton in July. The mission was unsuccessful, and on the return home HMS *Alceste* frigate, which conveyed it, was wrecked. After many privations and adventures the mission arrived at Batavia, and proceeded to England in HMS *Caesar*. St Helena was reached on 27 June 1817, and on 1 July Lord Amherst had a long interview with Napoleon, and afterwards presented his suite.

46. Sir Pulteney Malcolm, (1768-1838). Sir Pulteney entered the Royal Navy as a midshipman in 1778 and had a distinguished career. At the end of the war Sir Pulteney was appointed commander-in-chief of the St Helena station and succeeded Sir George Cockburn. He arrived in HMS *Newcastle* on 17 June 1816. he conducted himself with such firmness and gentleness combined, and so greatly to the satisfaction of Napoleon that the latter, while he discharged the whole brunt of his indignation upon the unlucky head of Sir Hudson Lowe, had an entirely different feeling for the admiral. "Ah! there is a man," he exclaimed, "with a countenance really pleasing: open, frank, and sincere. There is the face of an Englishman — his countenance bespeaks his heart; and I am sure he is a good man. I never yet beheld a man of whom I so immediately formed a good opinion as of that fine soldier-like old man. He carries his head erect, and speaks out openly and boldly what he thinks, without being afraid to look you in the face at the time. His physiognomy would make every person desirous of a further acquaintance, and render the most suspicious confident in him." Such was the striking portrait of Sir Pulteney drawn by the hand of a master — one who was the greatest of painters through the medium of language, as well as the first of epic poets by deed and action. On one occasion, when the impatient spirit of the exile burst forth, he exclaimed to the admiral, "Does your government mean to detain me upon this rock until my death's-day?" "Such, I apprehend, is their purpose," replied Sir Pulteney, calmly. "Then the term of my life will soon arrive," cried the indignant ex-sovereign. "I hope not, Sir," was the admiral's answer, "I hope you will survive to record your great actions, which are so numerous, and the task will insure you a term of long life." Napoleon bowed at this gratifying and well-merited compliment, and quickly resumed his good humour. Sir Pulteney continued in the command of the St Helena station from June 1816 till near the close of the following year; and when he left it he was on the best terms with Napoleon, who frequently afterwards used to speak of the pleasure he had enjoyed in his society. Sir Pulteney married, 1809, Clementina, daughter of William Fullerton Elphinstone; *see below.*

47. Whip — a mechanism, a hoist, for lowering things or people over the side of the ship.

48. Richard Guinness, (1792-1871). Guinness joined the Royal Society of Musicians in 1823, and was a well known leader of the orchestra at the Almack's balls.

49. John Fullerton Elphinstone, (1778-1854). Elphinstone was the son William Fullerton Elphinstone, (1740-1834). Elphinstone senior became Chairman of

the Court of Directors on three separate occasions, in 1804, 1806 and 1814, an unusual occurrence. He finally retired in 1826 and the age of 85. His knowledge and experience of Indian affairs was considered unrivalled. His eldest son, John Fullerton Elphinstone, using the benefit of family patronage accepted a position as writer for the H.E.I.C. in Canton in 1794, and remained there until his retirement in 1818, by which time he had become Chief representative of the Honorable East India Company in Canton. One of his sisters, Clementina, married, 1809, Admiral Sir Pulteney Malcom and is mentioned above.

50. There is no obvious record I have discovered showing that John Fullerton Elphinstone actually visited Napoleon, therefore his sister, Lady Clementina Malcolm may have conveyed the gift.

51. This brother was Major-General William George Keith Elphinstone, (1782-1842). He had a distinguished early career, but as an elderly, indecisive, weak, and unwell officer he proved himself utterly incompetent for his post in Afghanistan. His inability led to the disastrous British retreat from Kabul during January 1842, which saw his command all but wiped out in a massacre. Elphinstone died as a captive in Afghanistan some months later.

52. Saul Solomon, (1776-1852), the founder (1790) of a business house in St Helena. Saul, with his two brothers Lewis and Joseph, was engaged in business at Jamestown as a store-keeper and lodging-house keeper. His house was the resort of many who came to the Island, and in the days of the captivity news thus received from Europe was transmitted to the inhabitants of the Island. The house of Solomon was also frequently the medium through which clandestine correspondence was sent from Longwood to Europe. Solomon & Company (St Helena) Plc (or "Solomons" as it is known in Island households in 2012), has deep links to the history of St Helena, establishing it as an integral part of Island life. In 2012 with a staff complement of over 200 employees, the Company's activities cover a diverse range of businesses. Saul Solomon died in 1852, at Eastwood, Portishead, near Bristol, the residence of his son-in-law, Captain Thomas Montgomery Hunter.

53. Sir William Webber Doveton, as in note 36.

54. Sir John Leslie, (1766-1832), mathematician and natural philosopher. In 1810 Leslie improved on refrigeration techniques introducing a flat dish containing sulphuric acid under the receiver of an air-pump, with which device the acid absorbed the water vapour. The resulting air pump device could create ice.

55. Probably Miss De Fountain.

56. Captain James Wallis of HMS *Podargus* and HMS *Racoon*. He entered the Navy as captain's servant, and in 1797 was nominated Acting-Lieutenant. He was present in the Victory at the battle of Cape St Vincent, and, in 1804, was appointed First Lieutenant to the *Vincejo*, under the command of Captain John Wesley Wright. On 8 May 1804 this vessel was compelled to yield to superior force at the mouth of the Morbihan, and Wright and Wallis were detained in captivity. Wright met his death under unexplained circumstances in the Temple, but, in 1813, Wallis made his escape from Verdun. In August, 1814, Wallis was appointed Commander of the *Podargus* on the St Helena Station, and in 1817

he commanded the *Racoon*. After commanding the *Conqueror* for a short time in 1818, he returned to the *Racoon* and paid that ship off in 1818. It has been held to have been an act of bad taste on the part of the British Government to send Wallis to St Helena during Napoleon's captivity, but he was appointed to that station before it was decided to send the Emperor there. On 14 September 1817, O'Meara gives in his diary a conversation with Napoleon concerning the death of Wright, which was initiated by O'Meara mentioning that he had dined with Wallis the night before. Wallis died at Bridport, 21 September 1849.

57. Captain Henry Meynell, (1789-1865). Meynell was Commander of HMS *Newcastle*. During the year (17 June 1816 — 4 July 1817) that the *Newcastle* was on the St Helena Station, Captain Meynell frequently accompanied Admiral Sir Pulteney Malcolm when visiting Napoleon at Longwood, and his diary recording the conversations on these occasions was published in 1911. Meynell sat as MP for Lisburn, Ireland, from 1826 to 1847, and in 1862 he became full Admiral.

58. 'G.C.' was the Hon. George Carstairs. The other midshipman present at this date of 6 August 1816 (for there were two midshipmen who had been in conversation with Napoleon) was Francis H. Drake, son of Francis Drake (1764-1821), of Yardbury and Wells; a British diplomat, who had held positions at Genoa and Munich during the Napoleonic Wars.

59. Captain Henry Pierce Blakeney, 66th Regiment. Stationed at St Helena from 25 July 1817, to 16 July 1818.

60. The earthquake was on 21 September 1817.

61. HMS *Conqueror*, A 74-gun three-decker that had seen laid down in 1795, launched in 1801, was present at Trafalgar and decommissioned in 1820.

62. Dorothy Taubmann was Mark Wilks' second wife. After he died, she married, 1834, William Blamire (1790-1862), a farmer, civil servant and Liberal politician. Dorothy died in 1857.

63. Elizabeth Vassall Fox, Baroness Holland, (1771-1845). Both Lord and Lady Holland were admirers of Napoleon. In 1815, Lady Holland commission a bronze bust of him from sculptor Antonio Canova, which was placed in the garden at Holland House. After Napoleon was exiled to St Helena in 1815, Lady Holland sent him supplies of food and hundreds of books. Napoleon remembered Lady Holland in his will and following his death in 1821, his companions General Bertrand and the Marquis de Montholon arrived at Holland House, delivering a snuffbox. The gold snuffbox, which had been a gift to Napoleon from Pope Pius VI, was bequeathed by Lady Holland to the British Museum.

64. Charles James Fox, (1749-1806).

65. Louis Etienne St Denis, (1788-1856). The second valet at Longwood, and "Garde des Livres." He married Mary Hall, the governess, or nursemaid, to the children of the Countess Bertrand, and was at Longwood throughout the captivity. He returned in 1840 for the exhumation. Mary was selected by Lady Jerningham, and arrived on 26 June 1818. She married St Denis on 16 October 1819.

66. Rear-Admiral Robert Plampin, (1762-1834). Commander-in-Chief of the St Helena and Cape of Good Hope Naval Stations from July 1817, to July 1820. Plampin arrived in HMS *Conqueror* on 20 July 1817. He lived at the Briars after the Balcombe family left.

67. John Keats, *Endymion*.
    > ... And the dull twanging bowstring, and the raft
    > Branch down sweeping from a tall ash top,
    > Call'd up a thousand thoughts to envelope
    > Those who would watch.

68. Thomas Manning, (1772-1840). While at Cambridge, Manning became interested in the language and people of China, and in 1802 he went to Paris to study Chinese under Dr Hagar at the Biblothèque Nationale. There he became friendly with several scientists, and especially the elder Carnot, with whom he corresponded regularly on the subject of algebra. When war broke out between France and England in 1803 Carnot and Talleyrand are said to have persuaded Napoleon to allow Manning to return to England, which he did in 1805. Manning decided to go to Canton (Guangzhou) to perfect his Chinese, and in May 1806 obtained permission from the court of directors of the East India Company to travel there and live in the English factory as a doctor. He made several unsuccessful attempts to penetrate the interior of China and, with the exception of a visit to Cochin China in February 1808, stayed at Canton until 1810. Early that year he went to Calcutta, where for a few months, with his flowing beard, eccentric dress and manner, and witty conversation, he was the centre of society. Then, without government permission, with one Chinese servant, he set off and travelled as a doctor to Lhasa, where he arrived in December 1811, the first and for many years the only British traveller to reach the holy city. Ignoring the fact that he had been refused permission, he rode up to the *potala* (the Dalai Lama's palace), heavily but ineffectually disguised. Surprisingly he was permitted to stay for five months and was even granted an audience with the Dalai Lama, then a boy of seven.

    In 1816 Manning accompanied Lord Amherst's embassy to Peking as junior secretary and interpreter, despite Amherst's initial objection to his flowing beard as "incongruous" in a British embassy. When the embassy was over, he set off for home in the *Alceste*, but the ship was wrecked near Sunda on 17 February 1817. Continuing homeward in the *Caesar*, he reached St Helena, where he was granted an interview by Napoleon on 7 June 1817.

69. Brigadier-General Sir George Ridout Bingham, K.C.B., (1776-1833). Sir George arrived in HMS *Northumberland* and was in command of the troops in St Helena. He was an unofficial Member of Council, but the H.E.I.C. refused to confirm the appointment. He was appointed 21 May 1818 and retired 10 May 1819. He and Lady Bingham who arrived later lived at Knollcombe.

70. *Faute de mieux* — as a second best.

71. François Joseph Talma, (1763-1826). François Talma was born in Paris. His father, a dentist, moved to London, gave him a good English education. He returned to Paris, where for a year and a half he practised dentistry. His

predilection for the stage was cultivated in amateur theatricals, and on 21
November 1787 he made his debut at the Comédie-Française as Seide in
Voltaire's *Mahomet*. Talma married Julie Carreau, a rich and talented lady
whose salon attracted the principal Girondists. The actor was an intimate
friend of Napoleon, who delighted in his society, and even, on his return from
Elba, forgave him for performing before Louis XVIII. In 1808 the emperor had
taken him to Erfurt and made him play the *Mort de Cesar* to a company of
crowned heads. Five years later he took him to Dresden.

72. Denzil Ibbetson, (1788-1857). Ibbetson entered the Commissariat Department
    of the Army in 1808, and served in the Peninsular War. He sailed to St Helena
    on HMS *Northumberland* with Napoleon, and was one of only four officers to
    remain there for the duration of the captivity. He took over the job of purveying
    goods to Longwood House after William Balcombe fell out with the Governor
    and returned to England. He seems to have got on well with Hudson Lowe.
    He lived in the house at Hutts Gate vacated by the Bertrand family when they
    moved to their newly built cottage at Longwood.

    Denzil Ibbetson was a Commissary Officer on St Helena when Napoleon
    was exiled there from 1815 to 1821. Napoleon died in his residence the
    Longwood House on 5 May 1821 at the age of 51. Denzil Ibbetson was
    an accomplished artist and left diaries of his conversations with Napoleon and
    numerous sketches of Napoleon and the island. Denzil Ibbetson wrote on 7
    August 1815: "*Napoleon talks of invading England with 200,000 Infantry &
    6,000 Cavalry, but was uncertain of the disposition of the people of England,
    whether they would be for or against him, as he was induced to believe a great
    number would join him.*"

73. Mrs Baird was the wife of Captain James Baird, (1778-1848) of the 66th
    Regiment 1st Battalion.

74. Poniard — a short stabbing weapon; a dagger.

75. Baroness Sturmer, née Emmance de Boutet.

76. *Réveurs* — dreamers.